W9-CDX-498

AMERICAN ★ HEROES

AMERICAN HEROES

MARFÉ FERGUSON DELANO

NATIONAL GEOGRAPHIC

WASHINGTON, D.C.

CONTENTS

★ PROGRESSIVISM AND THE NEW DEAL ★
1900–1941 104

★ WAR, PROSPERITY, AND SOCIAL CHANGE ★
1941–PRESENT 138

What Is an American Hero?

ROBERT D. JOHNSTON

THE BEST HISTORIES ARE ABOUT HUMANITY. And with humanity comes heroism.

Americans have always, rightly, been attracted to the heroes of the past whether they be high-and-mighty generals who have directed our wars or the powerless who have thirsted for justice. For we can learn much by looking at the lives of heroes. We can see how people we admire made courageous ethical choices. We can see that it is possible to have the gumption to stand up in a crowd and make an unpopular decision. And we can see how individuals can make a real difference in human affairs.

Some scholars, though, say that looking for heroes in history is misguided—even dangerous. Focusing on extraordinary lives, they claim, makes us look up into the stratosphere, leading us to forget that it is ordinary people like us who make history.

In the aftermath of September 11, 2001, firefighters raise the American flag amid the smoldering ruins of the World Trade Center in New York City (left). The painting above portrays the legendary landing of the Pilgrims at Plymouth, Massachusetts, in 1620.

General George Washington held the poorly equipped and largely untrained troops of the Continental Army together for six years of fighting against the British. During the harsh and deadly winter at Valley Forge (above), he inspired his ragtag band to keep up the fight for freedom. At war's end in 1781, the grateful nation declared him a national hero.

Yet I don't think that's how historical heroes really work. Take Jackie Robinson, one of the biggest heroes in our baseball-obsessed house. My 17-year-old Sandy, and my 9-year-old Isaac, understand that they'll almost certainly never be as "great" as Robinson was. Yet they also draw the lesson from his life—from his heroism—that injustice is very much worth fighting and can be defeated through determination and dignity. They recognize, too, that Robinson, like many heroes, didn't really set out to be heroic— he just did what he felt he had to do.

American Heroes is a book that unapologetically brings us a whole host of historical heroes. Many if not most of them are familiar names, but author Marfé Ferguson Delano has done a remarkable job sketching parts of their lives both unfamiliar and intensely interesting.

How did Delano choose her all-star lineup? She and National Geographic consulted with librarians, a curriculum consultant, and with me, a historian who, among other things, trains future history teachers. It is tempting to say that part of our job wasn't too difficult. There are, after all, certain iconic individuals and moments that almost all Americans agree are truly heroic. Just look at the pictures illustrating the beginning of this book. George Washington and his frozen troops at Valley Forge. Marines raising the flag over Iwo Jima during World War II. New York firefighters at Ground Zero in the aftermath of September 11th.

But some of the other images are stranger, and even controversial. Women marching for the right to vote? One hundred years ago only a small minority of Americans would have found these suffragists heroic. And how about the pioneers in their covered wagons? My hunch is that most Americans still view these pioneers as heroes. Yet an increasing number of scholars and members of the public view them much less favorably, seeing the wagons as spearheads of a brutal eviction of Native Americans.

In the end, we generated this list of 50 profiles based on much debate and much compromise. It is not perfect, but it is meant to present a group of people,

This painting portrays the westward trek undertaken by pioneers as an idyllic journey. While many white settlers found a better life, it was at the expense of American Indians, who were forced to leave their native lands.

On March 3, 1913, more than 8,000 women marched in Washington, D.C., for a cause that many American women today take for granted: a woman's right to vote. As the participants marched from the U.S. Capitol to the White House, hostile spectators began to harass them. One police officer blamed the suffragists: "There would be nothing like this if you women would all stay at home," he said.

a group of great Americans, tested by time. They are not people whose feats of heroism come down to a single moment of bravery. They are heroes of history who can still speak to us today.

But "history" did not write this list, because "history" does not produce heroes. We generate our own heroes, looking into the past with our own values. These values, in turn, are different from year to year, decade to decade.

As the ethical ideals in this country have changed over time, so has what we might call "the face of the nation." Even before there was a United States, "America" was a vigorously multicultural

land. Still, until recently history textbooks have been written as if the only main actors in our past were elite white males. Fortunately, a greater inclusiveness has taken hold in the writing of American history. Therefore, *American Heroes* includes a blend that allows young readers to see those who look both similar to and different from themselves. Starting with Pocahontas and ending with Daniel Inouye, with Franklin Delano Roosevelt and Albert Einstein in between, the book does a masterful job pointing to the genuine diversity of heroes in American history.

If the combination of heroes in the book is complex, so too are the heroes

American pride ran high when astronaut Neil Armstrong became the first person to set foot on the moon on July 20, 1969. Two years later, astronaut James Irwin (above) took part in the first mission to use a lunar rover to explore the moon's surface. Space exploration requires a good deal of courage: Over the years, several astronauts have lost their lives during missions.

themselves. Those with stringent standards might ask for our heroes to be perfect, but this seems wrong. It is important to understand not only that all people are imperfect, but that even our heroes are people—people who have reached beyond their flaws to make exceptional contributions to humanity. George Washington owned many slaves; industrialist Andrew Carnegie sanctioned the killing of striking workers; and aviator Charles Lindbergh sympathized with Nazism. We may properly judge, and even condemn, them for these actions—after all, people at the time they lived did so. Yet we can still recognize the heroism that inspired Washington to

risk his life to lead his country to victory over the British; that led Carnegie to view his fortune as an instrument to help the world become more literate and peaceful; and that motivated Lindbergh to hazard a solo flight across the Atlantic. With humanity comes heroism, but with heroism also comes humanity.

In the end, because it is so well-written, and so important, I trust that *American Heroes* will find a wide audience. Marfé Ferguson Delano has given us a real gift—her ability to bring the past vividly and compellingly to life. I have a hunch that she understands that we not only care about the heroes in our history—we need them.

A NEW WORLD FROM MANY OLD WORLDS

★ *Beginnings–1763* ★

A diverse group of peoples from different continents played key roles in the making of America. When Christopher Columbus arrived in the West Indies in 1492, more than five million people lived on the land that is now Canada and the United States. These original inhabitants, now known as American Indians or Native Americans, lived in tribes, each of which had its own culture.

Pre-1492

Indian tribes thrived in North America long before Europeans arrived. Ancestral Puebloans (above) built multistoried dwellings in the Colorado Plateau more than a thousand years ago.

1587–1590

Roanoke Island's English settlement in today's North Carolina became the "Lost Colony." In 1590 a returning ship found no trace of the 115 colonists—only an Indian name, Croatoan, carved on a tree.

1619

Tobacco planters in Jamestown started the demand for African slaves (shown at auction, above). In the 1700s about 300,000 slaves were brought across the Atlantic to the North American mainland.

1754–1763

Defending their homelands, many American Indians joined forces with the French to fight against British soldiers and colonists in the battle for territory known as the French and Indian War.

The arrival of Columbus unleashed a series of events that, over the next four centuries, devastated American Indian life. His reports of the gold and other riches to be found in the New World lured more European explorers across the Atlantic. Spain, France, and Britain all claimed huge territories in North America and built colonies. Indians who resisted the invasion of their territory or who refused to cooperate with the colonists were often slaughtered. The greatest killers of all, however, were smallpox, measles, and other deadly diseases brought by Europeans. With no natural immunity to these illnesses, Indians died by the millions.

The first permanent British colony in North America was established in

———————— ★ ————————

"Your highnesses have an Other World here... from which such great wealth can be drawn."

CHRISTOPHER COLUMBUS TO SPAIN'S KING AND QUEEN, 1498

———————— ★ ————————

1607 at Jamestown, Virginia. The colonists prospered when they started growing tobacco, which became wildly popular in Europe. To get the farm labor they needed, Virginia's leaders turned to the slave trade. This brought—against their will—people from Africa to the New World. The first cargo of slaves arrived in Jamestown in 1619. Ironically, the first representative government in the New World, Virginia's House of Burgesses, was elected the same year.

Over the next century, thousands of colonists flocked to America. Some came seeking religious freedom; others came seeking fortunes. By 1732 the British had established 13 colonies along the east coast of North America. Most of the area's surviving American Indians were forced to move west.

Pocahontas

BORN	circa 1595, Virginia
DIED	March 1617, Gravesend, England
AGE AT DEATH	22?
OTHER NAMES	Matoaka, her Native American name; Rebecca, her baptized Christian name
FAMILY	Father: Powhatan, chief of Powhatan Tribal Confederacy in Virginia. Mother: unknown. Husband: colonist John Rolfe. He was ten years older than Pocahontas (poe-kuh-HAHNT-us). They married April 1614. Son: Thomas Rolfe, born 1615
LANDMARKS	Pocahontas was buried at the Church of St. George, Gravesend, Kent, England. Her grave has not been located, but memorial windows and a marker can be found there today.
MILESTONES	1616: Met King James I, England

Did You Know?

- The word *pocahontas* means "playful one." It was reported that as a young girl, Pocahontas was seen doing handsprings with young boys living at the Jamestown colony.
- Pocahontas may have acted as her father's ambassador, carrying messages from him to the colonists.
- The image of Pocahontas is on the flag and seal of Henrico County, Virginia.
- John Rolfe married again after Pocahontas died and lived in Virginia until his death in 1622. He crossed native tobacco with a milder variety—and created Virginia's first cash crop.
- Pocohontas's son, Thomas Rolfe became a wealthy tobacco farmer in Virginia.

ABOUT FOUR HUNDRED YEARS AGO, the young Indian princess Pocahontas became the first heroine in American history. As the story goes, she was about 12 years old when she saved the life of John Smith, one of the leaders of Virginia's Jamestown Colony. According to Smith, in December 1607 a group of Native Americans took him captive and brought him before their chief, Powhatan. Suddenly Smith's captors flung him down on a stone and stood "ready with their clubs to beat out his brains." In rushed Pocahontas, Powhatan's "dearest daughter," who took Smith's "head in her arms, and laid her own upon his to save him from death."

This story won Pocahontas a place in history for her kindheartedness and bravery, but it may be more legend than fact. The only record of the adventure is Smith's memoir, published 17 years after the alleged event. Details about Pocahontas's life are scarce, but historians believe that she was a frequent visitor to Jamestown. She and other members of Powhatan's tribe may have helped the English settlers survive during the long winters by bringing them food.

In 1613 the English kidnapped Pocahontas and held her hostage, hoping to convince Powhatan to release some English prisoners. During her captivity, Pocahontas became engaged to an English colonist named John Rolfe. After she converted to Christianity, they were married. The union brought about temporary goodwill between their peoples. In 1616 Pocahontas, Rolfe, and their infant son traveled to England, where she became a celebrity. The next year Pocahontas became ill and died at age 22. Today she is celebrated as a symbol of peace and friendship.

Famous for her legendary role in saving the life of Captain John Smith (left), Pocahontas was renamed Rebecca after her marriage to English colonist John Rolfe. Her 1616 trip to London, where the portrait above was painted, caused a sensation. She was even introduced to the king and queen of England.

ÆTIS.22.
1666.
OCTOBER 14

PAXQ

—B

William Penn

BORN	October 14, 1644, London, England
DIED	July 30, 1718, Buckinghamshire
AGE AT DEATH	73
FAMILY	Father: Admiral Sir William Penn. First wife: Gulielma Springett. When Gulielma died, he married Hannah Callowhill.
LANDMARKS	Penn founded Pennsylvania (which means "Penn's woods"), and he designed the capital, Philadelphia.
MILESTONES	1685: Quakers and political prisoners were released from jail because of Penn's growing influence in England. 1696: Penn drafted the first plan for unification of the American Colonies.

Did You Know?

- Penn was expelled from the University of Oxford for "religious unconformity."
- Penn wrote extensively on his beliefs, and he was imprisoned four times for his speeches and writings. He wrote *No Cross, No Crown* while imprisoned in the Tower of London and also recorded the first history of the Quaker religion, *A Brief Account of the Rise and Progress of the People Called Quakers.*
- Penn preached in Germany and Holland, which helped to encourage German and Dutch settlement of Pennsylvania.
- Penn's father was initially upset when Penn became a Quaker, but eventually reconciled with his son.
- Penn suffered a stroke in 1712.

WILLIAM PENN, FOUNDER OF THE PENNSYLVANIA COLONY, knew from his own experience what it was like to be persecuted for one's religious beliefs. He was a member of the Society of Friends, or Quakers. Quakers believe that each person has an "inward light" that allows direct communication with God. Most of them were pacifists who refused to take up arms in wars. In Penn's native England, Quakers and other dissenters risked fines, beatings, imprisonment, and even death for practicing their faith. Penn was thrown in prison four times for stating his beliefs in public.

In 1681 King Charles II gave Penn a large tract of land in America to repay a debt he owed Penn's father. Penn named the territory Pennsylvania. He knew exactly what he wanted to create there: a "holy experiment" where people would enjoy individual freedom, particularly the freedom to worship God as they pleased.

Penn helped draft Pennsylvania's Frame of Government, which guaranteed freedom of religion, trial by jury, and a representative government—ideas later found in the U.S. Constitution. Quakers and other persecuted groups flocked to the thriving colony.

In 1682 Penn made his first trip to his colony. Unlike other early founders, he tried to deal fairly with the Indians who lived there. He paid them for their lands, which helped foster peace between Indians and settlers.

Though he spent only a few years in his beloved colony, his commitment to religious tolerance and civil liberties mark William Penn as one of America's early heroes.

The son of a wealthy English Navy admiral, William Penn angered his father by becoming a Quaker when he was a young man. Even though the king of England had already given him the territory of Pennsylvania, Penn negotiated a price for the lands with the Indians who lived there (above). He later wrote of his colonial experiment, "Our Wilderness flourishes as a Garden."

Anne Hutchinson

BORN circa 1591, Lincolnshire, England

DIED 1643, Pelham Bay, New York

AGE AT DEATH 52?

OTHER NAMES Anne Marbury (maiden name)

FAMILY Married William Hutchinson, a merchant, in 1612. They had 15 children.

LANDMARKS Statue in front of the State House in Boston, Massachusetts

MILESTONES 1637: Her trial for violation of the laws of church and state

Did You Know?

- Hutchinson believed in a "covenant of grace," in which salvation could be achieved through grace alone. She thought prayers should not be memorized and believed anyone could have a personal relationship with God—a radical idea at the time.
- When Hutchinson lived in Boston, as many as 80 people came to her weekly meetings.
- An admirer praised her as "a woman who preaches better gospel than any of your black-coats who have been at the ninnyversity."
- She said, "I feel that nothing important ever happens that is not revealed to me beforehand."
- Anne Hutchinson defended herself at trial with these words: "As I understand it, laws...are for those who have not the light which makes plain the pathway." Her authority to preach, she claimed, came from this inner light.
- Harvard University was founded in 1636 in part in response to the preaching and activities of Anne Hutchinson.

When Anne Hutchinson immigrated to Massachusetts Bay Colony, she hoped it would be a place where she could express her religious beliefs freely. She soon found that the colony's leaders were as intolerant of religious dissent as the government in her native England. But she didn't let that stop her from practicing her faith as she chose.

Anne, a skilled midwife, and her merchant husband, William, settled in Boston in 1634. Like most of the colony's settlers, they were Puritans. Anne had her own ideas about worship, however. She believed that people didn't need ministers to help them communicate with God. When she began holding prayer meetings, many people came to hear her preach.

Anne's teachings alarmed Governor John Winthrop and the colony's powerful religious leaders. They worried that she might influence other women to rebel against their traditional role. In 1637 Anne was charged with violating the laws of church and state. At her trial, she defended herself with courage and eloquence.

Despite this, the court found Anne guilty and banished her and her family from Massachusetts. They moved to what is now Rhode Island and later to present-day New York, where she was killed by Native Americans.

Anne Hutchinson not only defended her faith, she refused to yield to male authority at a time when women were expected to obey men. By doing so, she helped set the stage for religious freedom and women's rights in America.

Religious reformer Anne Hutchinson impressed Governor John Winthrop as "a woman of haughty and fierce carriage, a nimble wit and active spirit, a very voluble tongue, more bold than a man." Six years after he expelled her from Massachusetts, she and her children were killed by Indians in New York—an event imagined in gruesome detail in the drawing above.

A REVOLUTIONARY AGE

★ *1763–1789* ★

In little more than a decade, the American colonists went from being loyal subjects of the British crown to rebels fighting for independence. When the Seven Years' War (known in America as the French and Indian War) ended in 1763, most colonists were proud to have helped Great Britain achieve victory over France and its allies. But relations between the colonies and the motherland soon took a turn for the worse.

1773

Boston Tea Party: On December 16, American Patriots dressed as Indians boarded British East India Company ships and dumped their cargoes of tea into Boston Harbor in protest of the British tax on tea.

1776

On July 4 the Declaration of Independence was adopted by the Continental Congress. John Hancock, who served as president of the Congress, was first to sign his name to the document.

1781

The final battle of the Revolutionary War ended on October 19 when British general Charles Cornwallis surrendered his army to General George Washington at Yorktown, Virginia.

1787

Members of the Constitutional Convention debated what kind of government the new nation should have. Benjamin Franklin (left) helped persuade most of the delegates to sign the Constitution.

Colonists resented the restrictions Britain placed on settling lands west of the Appalachians. They were even more offended when the British parliament taxed them to cover the huge expense of fighting the recent war. American leaders spoke out against taxation without representation, and popular resistance to British rule began to grow.

Eventually, colonial resistance bloomed into outright rebellion. The first shots of the American Revolution were fired in April 1775. A year later, "the Thirteen United States of America" cut their colonial ties with Great Britain and proclaimed themselves part of a brand new country. It took courage for

★

"We hold these truths to be self-evident, that all men are created equal...."

DECLARATION OF INDEPENDENCE, 1776

★

delegates to sign the Declaration of Independence: The penalty for disloyalty to the crown was death. Along with the challenge of defeating the most powerful nation on earth, Americans faced the daunting task of organizing a new government that reflected their democratic ideals. Victory over Britain came in 1781. Devising a strong and stable government took several years longer.

The Founding Fathers of revolutionary times have become some of America's most beloved heroes. We honor their commitment to liberty and equality and their efforts to create our country. They were men of their times, however, with different values from those many hold today. As such, their democratic vision did not extend to the entire population. Many of the revolutionaries were slaveholders, and hardly any of them even considered women's lack of rights.

Benjamin Franklin

BORN	January 17, 1706, Boston, Massachusetts
DIED	April 17, 1790, Philadelphia, Pennsylvania
AGE AT DEATH	84
OTHER NAMES	Silence Dogood, Richard Saunders, Poor Richard
FAMILY	Father: Josiah Franklin. Mother: Abiah Folger. Common-law wife: Deborah Read. Three children: William (mother unknown), Sarah, and Francis Folger (died age 4, of smallpox)
LANDMARKS	Christ Church (grave); the Franklin Institute, Philadelphia, Pennsylvania
HONORS	1753: Copley Medal from Britain's Royal Society for his work in electricity. 1766: Elected member of Royal Society of Sciences

Did You Know?

- Ben Franklin was still teaching swimming in his seventies. He is the only Founding Father in the Swimming Hall of Fame.
- Franklin invented many items, including bifocals and the lightning rod. The famous composer Mozart wrote two pieces for Franklin's musical invention, the glass armonica, which produced sound through vibrating glass spheres.
- When in school, Franklin did not do well in math classes. He learned best through experience. He did, however, teach himself to read in five languages: German, French, Spanish, Italian, and Latin.
- Franklin's son, William, became the colonial governor of New Jersey and remained loyal to Great Britain during the American Revolution, which led to an estrangement with his father. William was arrested in 1776 and lived out the rest of his life in England.

PRINTER, AUTHOR, POSTMASTER, businessman, scientist, inventor, musician, patriot, diplomat, and international celebrity. All of these labels—and more—fit Benjamin Franklin, America's most versatile Founding Father and one of the most remarkable men the world has ever known.

Born in Boston, Benjamin was the 15th child of Josiah Franklin, a poor candle- and soapmaker. When Ben was ten years old his father put him to work in his shop. Ben hated the hot and smelly business. But he loved books and reading and writing, so his father decided to apprentice him to his older brother James, a printer.

Ben learned how to set type and run the press, and he read everything that came his way. To save money to buy books of his own, and to improve his health, he stopped eating costly meat and for several years was a vegetarian. To better his writing skills, he studied essays by authors he admired and practiced writing in the same style. Teenage Ben's commitment to self-improvement—of mind, body, and behavior—would last his entire life. Later in life he came up with a set of 13 virtues to aim for and a system of practicing them. He admitted he did not live up to his own ideals, but he noted that the attempt to do so made him "a better and a happier Man than I otherwise should have been."

When he was 16, Ben wrote a series of clever articles for the newspaper James published. He recalled in his autobiography: "But being still a Boy, and suspecting that my Brother would object to printing any Thing of

One of America's most beloved Founding Fathers, Benjamin Franklin valued freedom above all else. "They that can give up essential liberty to obtain a little temporary safety," he wrote in 1759, "deserve neither liberty nor safety." As a printer (above) and writer, Franklin understood the important role a free press played in society.

Benjamin Franklin's famous electricity experiment in 1752 became the stuff of American legend. This 19th-century print shows Franklin, assisted by his son, William, launching a kite with a key attached to it as a thunderstorm brews in the background. The experiment proved that lightning and electricity were one and the same. Franklin used the knowledge to perfect the lightning rod, which he considered his most important invention.

mine in his Paper if he knew it to be mine, I contriv'd to disguise my Hand, and writing an anonymous Paper I put it in at Night under the Door of the Printing-House." Ben signed his essays with the pseudonym, or false name, of Silence Dogood. It was the first of many pseudonyms he would use during his long career as a writer.

Ben often quarreled with his brother, perhaps because, as he later admitted, "[I was] too saucy and provoking." When he was 17, he ran away from Boston. He ended up in Philadelphia and soon landed a job in a print shop.

Eager to see more of the world, Franklin jumped at an offer to sail to London in 1724.

Franklin published this political cartoon in 1754 to encourage the American Colonies to unite against frontier raids by the French and their Indian allies.

Once there, he used his printing skills to support himself. In his spare time he explored the big city and swam in the River Thames. Few people knew how to swim in those days, and Franklin enjoyed showing off. He taught his friends how to swim, and as a boy had invented finlike paddles for his hands and feet to increase his speed.

Franklin was always enormously curious about the world around him. On his voyage back to America in 1726, he spent hours studying the sea. On another voyage, he measured the ocean's temperature as the ship progressed. He observed that the water in the large current known as the Gulf Stream was almost 20 degrees warmer than the surrounding sea. Other Atlantic crossings later in life let Franklin further probe the secrets of the Gulf Stream. By tracking the sea's temperature, he helped chart the course of the "river in the ocean."

Franklin's intense curiosity was equaled by his lifelong desire to be useful to his fellow human beings. He had the Gulf Stream engraved on maps, so that ship captains could use the information to improve the speed of their vessels. Staying in the current sped their journey on eastward voyages, and avoiding it helped them make better time when traveling west.

Back in Philadelphia, Franklin focused his energies on the printing and publishing business. Within a few years the hardworking young man had acquired his own printing shop and his own newspaper, the *Pennsylvania Gazette.* He had also fathered a son, William, with a woman whose name he never revealed. When Deborah Read became Franklin's wife in 1730, William was part of their family. They later had two more children.

Among the 13 virtues that Franklin identified was Industry: "Lose no time.—Be always employ'd in something useful." Franklin seems to have followed this advice. Over the next two decades, he expanded his printing business into several other cities, and he became the official printer for the colony of Pennsylvania. He was also appointed the postmaster of Philadelphia. To help improve life for himself and others, Franklin also founded the first lending library in the Colonies, as well as Philadelphia's first fire company, a public hospital, and a militia.

Although Franklin thought of himself primarily as a printer, he was also a prolific writer. He penned articles, editorials, pamphlets, thousands of letters, and an autobiography. Franklin launched his best known publication, *Poor Richard's Almanack,* in 1732. Published annually for

Note, This ALMANACK us'd to contain but 24 Pages, and now has 36 ; yet the Price is very little advanc'd.

Poor RICHARD improved :

BEING AN

ALMANACK

AND

EPHEMERIS

OF THE

MOTIONS of the SUN and MOON;

THE TRUE

PLACES and ASPECTS of the PLANETS ;

THE

RISING and SETTING of the SUN;

AND THE

Rising, Setting *and* Southing *of the* Moon,

FOR THE

BISSEXTILE YEAR, 1748.

Containing also,

The Lunations, Conjunctions, Eclipses, Judgment of the Weather, Rising and Setting of the Planets, Length of Days and Nights, Fairs, Courts, Roads, &c. Together with useful Tables, chronological Observations, and entertaining Remarks.

Fitted to the Latitude of Forty Degrees, and a Meridian of near five Hours West from London ; but may, without sensible Error, serve all the NORTHERN COLONIES.

By RICHARD SAUNDERS, Philom.

PHILADELPHIA:

Printed and Sold by B. FRANKLIN.

Writing under the pen name of Poor Richard, Franklin enlightened and entertained the colonies with Poor Richard's Almanack. *First published in 1732, the publication helped make Franklin a wealthy man.*

"If you wou'd not be forgotten,
As soon as you are
dead and rotten,
Either write things
worth reading,
Or do things worth the writing"

Poor Richard's Almanack, 1738

"We must all hang together, or assuredly we shall all hang separately."

Reportedly said by Franklin at the signing of Declaration of Independence, July 4, 1776

25 years, the book featured farming and weather information, financial advice, and clever, witty sayings, such as "Fish and visitors smell after three days." It was a huge success, and it made Franklin's name a household word in the Colonies.

Poor Richard also helped make Franklin rich. In 1748, at the age of 42, he retired from printing. He wanted to devote the rest of his life to his two main passions: scientific research and public service.

The mysterious force of nature known as electricity fascinated Franklin. He theorized that lightning and electricity were one and the same, and then proved it one night in 1752 by flying a kite with a key attached to it during a thunderstorm. His discoveries in electricity gave people a new understanding of the force. Word of his experiments spread throughout England and Europe, bringing him international fame.

Franklin put his scientific knowledge to work in ways that could help others. He invented the lightning rod, which helped protect buildings and ships from dangerous lightning strikes. Among his other practical inventions were bifocal glasses and a smokeless fireplace. Franklin never patented any of his inventions. He believed that "As we benefit from the inventions of others, we should be glad to share our own."

In the 1750s, Franklin became more involved in politics. He was elected to

One of Franklin's favorite inventions was the glass armonica, a musical instrument that produced sound through vibrating glass spheres. He enjoyed playing it for friends.

the Pennsylvania legislature, and he began to voice objections to England's treatment of the Colonies, especially to what he viewed as unfair taxation.

From 1757 to 1762 Franklin served in London as the agent of the Pennsylvania Assembly, and he lobbied for the colonists' rights. He sailed to England again in 1764. This time he also represented the colonies of Georgia, New Jersey, and Massachusetts. He tried to prevent passage of the unpopular Stamp Act, and when he failed he began a propaganda campaign, writing dozens of pieces against the tax. His efforts led to the repeal of the Stamp Act a year after it was passed.

Franklin stayed in England for about a decade, trying but ultimately failing to negotiate more rights and freedom for the 13 Colonies. He concluded American independence was inevitable.

While Franklin was sailing home in April 1775, war broke out at the battles of Lexington and Concord. Franklin became a leader in this American Revolution. He represented Pennsylvania in the Second Continental Congress, where he was one of the first delegates to advocate complete independence from Great Britain. In 1776, 70-year-old Franklin helped draft the Declaration of Independence.

The new nation needed friends to help it defeat the powerful English army and navy, and Franklin was sent to France to find them. The French greeted the famous scientist-turned-

Benjamin Franklin (above left with John Adams and Thomas Jefferson) reviewed Jefferson's draft of the Declaration of Independence. He was the only Founding Father to sign it, the Constitution, and the Treaty of Paris, which formally ended the Revolutionary War. When Franklin went to France in 1776, the French—agog over his scientific achievements—welcomed him warmly. In 1778 he was presented to King Louis XVI at Versailles (above right).

famous scientist-turned-diplomat with great enthusiasm. Franklin was flattered by all the attention. He wrote to his daughter, "My picture is everywhere, on the lids of snuff boxes, on rings, busts....Your father's face is now as well known as the man in the moon."

The French agreed to help the Americans against the British. For the next nine years, Franklin stayed in France, representing the 13 United States of America and helping to organize the war effort. In 1783 he helped negotiate a peace treaty with Great Britain that granted full independence to the American Colonies.

In 1785, Benjamin Franklin made his last Atlantic crossing. In Philadelphia, he was hailed a hero. At age 81, he represented Pennsylvania at the Constitutional Convention in Philadelphia. His impassioned support of the Constitution helped persuade most delegates to sign the document.

Franklin stayed busy until the end of his life. In his final years, he penned his autobiography. He also took up the antislavery cause. Franklin, like most of the other Founding Fathers, was a slave owner. But he eventually came to look at slavery as "an atrocious debasement of human nature." He joined an abolitionist group and made plans to free his two slaves. And he spoke up for the need to educate freed slaves, which he believed would "promote the public good, and the happiness of these hitherto much neglected fellow-creatures." Mindful of all his fellow creatures until the end, Benjamin Franklin died on

Thomas Paine

BORN	January 29, 1737, Thetford, England
DIED	June 8, 1809, New York, New York
AGE AT DEATH	72
FAMILY	Father: Joseph Pain. Paine added an "e" to his name once he came to America. Mother: Frances Cocke. Two brief marriages
MILESTONES	1776: "Common Sense" published. December 1793–November 1794: Jailed in France

Did You Know?

- Paine was also an inventor. He concentrated on developing an iron bridge and a smokeless candle.
- Paine was imprisoned during the French Revolution for favoring the banishment of King Louis XVI rather than his execution.
- Paine held many jobs during his life, including corsetmaker, tax collector, and clerk of the Pennsylvania General Assembly.
- Paine dedicated the "Rights of Man" to George Washington. In his "Part the Second" to the "Rights of Man," Paine discusses a state that would take care of its citizens with public employment for the poor and retirement benefits.
- By the end of the Revolution, more than half a million copies of "Common Sense" had been printed and sold.
- After coming to America, Paine traveled back and forth to Europe two times.
- Paine's bones were exhumed from New York State to be taken for burial in England, but they were lost and never recovered.

WHEN THOMAS PAINE ARRIVED IN AMERICA in November 1774, the aim of most liberty-loving Americans was to gain their full rights as Englishmen. Only a few had American independence as their goal. That began to change in 1776, thanks in great part to "Common Sense," a political pamphlet written by Paine that served as a wake-up call for the colonists.

Compared to rich and powerful men such as George Washington, Thomas Jefferson, and Benjamin Franklin, Tom Paine was an unlikely Founding Father. He lived much of his life in poverty. Born in Thetford, England in 1737, he was the son of a corsetmaker, a craftsman who made women's undergarments. He attended school for about seven years, then at age 13 he began to work with his father in his corset shop.

Over the next 24 years Paine moved on to a number of other occupations, including sailor and tax officer, but he was not very happy or successful in any of them. In 1774 Paine was fired from his job as a tax officer, and he and his second wife separated. His future looked bleak until he ran into Benjamin Franklin *(see pages 22–27)* in London. Franklin encouraged him to seek a new life in America and gave him a letter of introduction. That October, Paine set sail for Philadelphia.

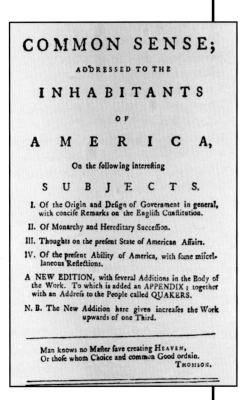

COMMON SENSE;

ADDRESSED TO THE

INHABITANTS

OF

AMERICA,

On the following interesting

SUBJECTS.

I. Of the Origin and Design of Government in general, with concise Remarks on the English Constitution.

II. Of Monarchy and Hereditary Succession.

III. Thoughts on the present State of American Affairs.

IV. Of the present Ability of America, with some miscellaneous Reflections.

A NEW EDITION, with several Additions in the Body of the Work. To which is added an APPENDIX; together with an Address to the People called QUAKERS.

N. B. The New Addition here given increases the Work upwards of one Third.

Man knows no Master save creating HEAVEN,
Or those whom Choice and common Good ordain.
THOMSON.

Thomas Paine is regarded as one of the most successful political propagandists of all time. His pamphlets: "Common Sense" (above) and "The American Crisis" inspired American colonists to fight for independence. In "Common Sense," Paine called King George III a "royal brute." More than 100,000 copies of the pamphlet sold in the six months leading up to the Declaration of Independence.

An editorial cartoon shows Tom Paine having a nightmare in which three judges unfurl a list of charges and punishments against him, while a gallows and stock loom in the background. The cartoon reflects the fact that Paine's call for American independence was treasonous to the crown, an offense punishable by death. Paine's writings caused him to be denounced by the British as a traitor in 1792. He was tried in absentia and became an outlaw in England, the land of his birth.

Once there, he soon found work as an editor. He also became acquainted with a small group of rebels advocating American independence. Paine took their cause to heart, and in January 1776 he published "Common Sense," believed by some historians to be one of the most influential pieces of political propaganda ever written.

In "Common Sense," Paine attacked not only British rule but the very idea of a monarchy. A king, he wrote, is "nothing better than the principal ruffian of some restless gang....Of more worth is one honest man to society and in the sight of God, than all the crowned ruffians that ever lived." He went on to argue for independence

and to outline a form of government in which people would rule themselves in a direct way—a democracy. In closing he suggested that an independent America was the only hope for humanity: "Ye that dare oppose, not only the tyranny but the tyrant, stand forth! Every spot of the Old World is overrun with oppression. Freedom hath been hunted round the globe....O! receive the fugitive and prepare in time an asylum for mankind."

Written in a bold yet simple style, "Common Sense" quickly became a best seller. Colonists from Maine to Georgia bought more than 100,000 copies in the six months leading up to the Declaration of Independence. Paine's impassioned words persuaded many Americans that the time had come to break free from Britain and create a new nation of their own.

Paine threw himself into the revolutionary cause. He donated his share of the profits from "Common Sense" to buy supplies for the Continental Army, and then joined the Army himself. He was with General Washington *(see pages 32–35)* in December 1776, when his troops were on the verge of falling apart after being chased into Pennsylvania by the redcoats. To help boost American spirits, Paine penned "The American Crisis," which opened with these famous words: "These are the times that try men's souls. The summer soldier and the sunshine patriot will, in this crisis, shrink from the service of his country; but he that stands it now, deserves the love and thanks of man and woman. Tyranny, like Hell, is not easily conquered; yet we have this consolation with us, that the harder the conflict, the more glorious the triumph." Washington had the pamphlet read aloud to his troops, who were inspired to fight on.

This engraving depicts Thomas Paine holding a scroll representing the "Rights of Man"—a pamphlet he published in England in 1791 in response to criticism of the French Revolution. The work called for social reform and appealed to the English to overthrow their monarchy and establish a republic.

After the war Paine found himself penniless once again. He found it hard to get work, in part because he had developed a reputation for being indiscreet and egotistical. In 1787 he returned to England, where he published another best-selling pamphlet, the "Rights of Man," in two parts in 1791 and 1792. A defense of the French Revolution, the work earned him a charge of "seditious libel." To avoid arrest, Paine fled to France, where he was soon imprisoned for speaking out against the execution of King Louis XVI. In prison he wrote his "Age of Reason," which criticized organized religion and earned him enemies on both sides of the Atlantic.

Paine returned to America in 1802 and settled on a farm in New Rochelle, New York. Treated as an outcast for his religious views, he spent the last years of his life sad, sick, poor, and often drunk. When he died in 1809, only six mourners attended his funeral. Today, Paine's reputation has been restored as a brilliant thinker and writer who was a driving force in America's move toward independence.

"There is something absurd in supposing a continent to be perpetually governed by an island."

"Common Sense," January 10, 1776

George Washington

Did You Know?

- While the legend of Washington chopping down a cherry tree and then confessing to his father illustrates Washington's character, historians think it never happened.
- Washington only traveled outside the United States once—to Barbados.
- Washington did not have wooden teeth, but he did have several sets of false teeth.
- Washington declared the nation's first Thanksgiving, October 3, 1789.
- According to Washington's birth record, he had no middle name.

CALLED THE "FATHER OF HIS COUNTRY," George Washington is best known today for being the first President of the United States. But Washington deserves equal honor for his courage and skill as a military leader. As the commanding general of America's Continental Army, he led the 13 Colonies to victory during the Revolutionary War. Had the Americans failed to defeat the British, the United States as we know it would not exist.

Washington was the son of a Virginia landowner and planter. When he was 16 he found work as a surveyor and set off to chart the wilds of Virginia's Shenandoah Valley.

Washington joined the Virginia militia at the age of 22 and became a lieutenant colonel. He fought for the British in the French and Indian War. During one battle, two horses were shot from under him and bullets flew through his coat, but somehow he escaped without injury. Brave and calm in the face of danger, Washington gained the respect and loyalty of his men. His reputation as a gifted leader spread throughout the colonies.

When he was 26, Washington retired from military service. For the next 17 years, he devoted himself to managing his Virginia plantation, Mount Vernon, which he ran with slave labor. He also served in Virginia's colonial legislature. In 1759, he married Martha Dandridge Custis, a wealthy widow with two young children.

Meanwhile, resistance to British rule began to grow in the Colonies. Washington was one of those who thought that British demands and taxes were unfair. In a July

The first President of the United States, George Washington is honored today in countless ways—from monuments across the country to the many schools and towns named for him to his image on both the one-dollar bill and the quarter (above). He is the only President to have a state named for him.

While he was still a teenager, George Washington worked as a surveyor, measuring and mapping the unsettled wilderness of Virginia's Shenandoah Valley (above left). As a young man, he fought on the western frontier for the British in the French and Indian War. During that conflict Washington learned much about military strategy and organization from British officers. As commander-in-chief of the Continental Army, he turned this knowledge against the British during the Revolutionary War. He finally forced the British to surrender at Yorktown, Virginia, in 1781 (above right).

1774 letter he wrote, "I think the Parliament of Great Britain hath no more Right to put their hands into my Pocket, without my consent, than I have to put my hands into your's, for money." When Washington attended the Second Continental Congress as a delegate from Virginia in May 1775, the first shots of the American war for independence had already been fired. The delegates chose George Washington to lead the new Continental Army against the British.

The troops of the Continental Army were poorly equipped and largely untrained, but Washington held them together for six years of fighting against the world's most powerful empire. He decided early on that the best strategy was to avoid major battles whenever possible and to harass the British instead. He used surprise attacks and organized a spy network to outfox the enemy. Washington's courage and commitment to the revolutionary cause inspired the ragtag American army. With help from the French, Washington forced the British to surrender in October 1781.

Washington again retired from military service in 1783 and returned to Mount Vernon. His stay there, however, lasted just a few years. The new nation he had helped create was in danger of falling apart. Washington realized that the federal government needed to be strengthened if the United States was to survive. In May 1787, he gathered in Philadelphia with delegates from other

"Observe good faith and justice toward all nations.
Cultivate peace and harmony with all...."

Farewell Address, September 17, 1796

This famous painting of General George Washington crossing the icy Delaware River to lead an attack on the British captures his heroic role in American history. The fate of the new nation depended in large part on him—first as commander-in-chief of the Continental Army and then as the nation's first President. A legend in his own time, George Washington remains one of America's most enduring heroes.

states for a meeting that came to be known as the Constitutional Convention. By September the delegates had written the new Constitution of the United States. After the document was ratified by the states, the nation's first presidential election took place.

George Washington, the war hero, was everyone's first choice for President. He was elected unanimously by a group of electors in the nation's first electoral college. He journeyed to New York, which was then the nation's capital, and he took the oath of office on April 30, 1789. An account from the time noted of Washington: "There was in his whole appearance an unusual dignity and gracefulness which at once secured him profound respect, and cordial esteem. He seemed born to command his fellow men."

Washington did his best to live up to the trust his country had placed in him. He knew that everything he did in office would set a precedent,

George Washington first took the oath of office in New York City on April 30, 1789. He was twice elected by unanimous vote.

or model, for future presidents to follow. He used his powers as President to appoint Cabinet members and judges, to command the armed forces, and to negotiate treaties. He left it to Congress to make laws, as provided for in the Constitution. President Washington was so popular that he was reelected unanimously.

By the end of his second term, Washington had grown weary of politics. In his farewell address, he urged his fellow citizens to avoid splitting into political parties and to strive for unity: "With slight shades of difference you have the same religion, manner, habits, and political principles."

In 1797, George and Martha Washington returned to Mount Vernon. Less than three years later, Washington died of a throat infection at age 67. The entire nation mourned for months the man praised as "first in war, first in peace, and first in the hearts of his countrymen."

Abigail Adams

Did You Know?

• Abigail came from a wealthy Massachusetts family. Like most girls in the 18th century, she had no formal schooling. She read widely, however, and early on drew admiration for her wit and lively intelligence.

• More than 2,000 of Adams's letters survive. Historians find them a valuable source of information about her husband and the country.

• In Abigail's famous "Remember the Ladies" letter, she warned her husband: "If particular care and attention is not paid to the ladies we are determined to foment a rebellion, and will not hold ourselves bound by any laws in which we have no voice, or representation." Her husband's response was not particularly encouraging: "As to your extraordinary Code of Laws, I cannot but laugh."

• Adams spent almost a year in France, where she was disturbed by the luxuries of Paris. She did, however, grow more tolerant of the French.

ABIGAIL ADAMS WAS THE WIFE of one President and the mother of another. She was also a remarkable woman in her own right.

In 1764 Abigail married a young lawyer named John Adams. He became a leader in the American Revolution, and in 1774 he was appointed to the First Continental Congress in Philadelphia. Abigail stayed in Massachusetts with their five children. She ran the family farm and oversaw business affairs.

For most of the next ten years Abigail and John lived apart, but they stayed connected through letters. They wrote of their love and their children, and they exchanged ideas on religion, philosophy, and politics.

Like her husband, Abigail strongly supported American independence. Her ideas on equality, however, surpassed his. In a letter written to John in March 1776, she made a bold claim for women's rights: "in the new Code of Laws...I desire you would Remember the Ladies, and be more generous and favourable to them than your ancestors...."

After the war, Abigail joined her husband as he served as a diplomat, as George Washington's Vice President, and then as the second President of the United States. Over the years she sent her family and friends thousands of letters in which she chronicled her life and times. Today Abigail Adams is honored for her intellect, her independent spirit, her vivid letter-writing skills, and her forward-looking ideas about politics and women's rights.

At a time when women had no political rights, Abigail Adams did not hesitate to share her opinions about how the new nation should be governed. She expressed her ideas in lively letters to family and friends. Among the recipients of her letters (above) was Thomas Jefferson, whom she took to task for criticizing her husband's actions as President.

THE NEW REPUBLIC

★ *1789–1848* ★

The one thing nearly all Americans agreed about in the early days of the new republic was their deep respect for President George Washington. But not long after his election, members of his own Cabinet began to clash over the role the federal government should play in the affairs of the nation and in foreign affairs. During Washington's second term, two political parties began to form.

1793

After Eli Whitney's cotton gin made processing cotton fast and profitable, huge tracts of land in the South were planted with the crop. The South became more dependent than ever on slave labor.

1807

Inventor Robert Fulton launched the first successful steamboat, the Claremont, *on the Hudson River in 1807. Far faster than sailboats, steamboats were soon transporting freight and passengers.*

1812

Fur trader Robert Stuart found a 20-mile-wide gap through the Rockies—a key part of the Oregon Trail. In the 1840s and '50s, hundreds of thousands of settlers migrated along westbound trails.

1836

After suffering a crushing defeat at the Battle of the Alamo (above), American settlers in Texas gained independence from Mexico in April 1836.

When the nation's second President, John Adams, a Federalist, ran for reelection in 1800, his opponent was Thomas Jefferson, a Democratic-Republican. Despite the bitter rivalry between the two men, Adams accepted the outcome when Jefferson won. The peaceful transfer of power from one leader to the next signaled that America's experiment in democracy was off to a good start.

The United States doubled in size in 1803, with the purchase of the Louisiana Territory. Over the next 45 years, the United States expanded to the Pacific Ocean. The nation's democratic ideals did not protect the native inhabitants of these regions, however. As land-hungry white settlers surged westward,

---------------- ★ ----------------

*"The excellence of every government
is its adaptation to the state
of those to be governed by it."*

THOMAS JEFFERSON, LETTER OF 1816

---------------- ★ ----------------

Indian tribes were driven out. Some fought to the death rather than give up their way of life. African-American slaves were also shut out of the new democracy. Although antislavery thinking was gaining power in the North, politically powerful Southern slave owners clung to the brutal institution that made them rich. This conflict would soon threaten the very existence of the nation.

Despite these problems, the achievements of the American people during these decades are impressive. They built roads, railways, canals, cities, and factories; cleared forests and tended farms; and explored vast wildernesses. Along the way, they began to create a uniquely American culture and way of life.

George Mason

BORN December 11, 1725, Fairfax County, Virginia

DIED October 7, 1792, Fairfax County, Virginia

AGE AT DEATH 66

FAMILY Married Anne Eilbeck in 1750. Their first son, George Jr., was born three years later. They had 12 children, but three died in infancy. Anne died at age 39. In 1780 he married Sarah Brent.

LANDMARKS George Mason Memorial, Washington, D.C. Gunston Hall Plantation, Mason Neck, Virginia

Did You Know?

- Mason helped draft the Constitution of the Commonwealth of Virginia and the U.S. Constitution.
- Mason was a partner in the Ohio Company, a business that bought and sold land.
- Mason took great pride in his ability as a grower of fruit and nut trees. Among others, cherry and English walnut trees graced his Virginia estate, Gunston Hall.
- Mason's poor health caused him to decide not to fill a vacancy in the U.S. Senate.
- In addition to Gunston Hall, Mason owned some 24,000 acres in both Virginia and neighboring Maryland.
- Thomas Jefferson referred to Mason as the wisest man of his generation.
- Northern Virginia is home to a university named for Mason, George Mason University.

THOUGH HE IS NOT ONE OF AMERICA'S better known Founding Fathers, few people had a more lasting influence on our nation than George Mason. For it is largely due to him that the U.S. Constitution contains our cherished Bill of Rights.

Mason was born in 1725 to a wealthy Virginia planter and his wife. When he was ten years old his father died. His uncle, who owned one of the largest book collections in the Colonies, saw to it that he received an excellent education. In 1750 Mason married Anne Eilbeck, who bore him 12 children. His Virginia plantation, Gunston Hall, was just down the Potomac River from Mount Vernon, which belonged to his friend George Washington (*see pages 32–35*).

Over the years Mason took part in local politics, and he became widely respected for his knowledge of the law. In the 1760s, Mason helped lead Virginia's protest against "taxation without representation." He eventually became one of Virginia's leading supporters of American independence.

In the spring of 1776 Mason was elected to the fifth Virginia Convention, which was held in the colonial capital of Williamsburg. Delayed by illness, he arrived almost two weeks late. By that time the delegates had already voted unanimously "to declare the United Colonies free and independent States." But there was still plenty of work to do. The new Commonwealth of Virginia needed a "Declaration of Rights, and such a plan of Government as will be most likely to maintain peace and order in this Colony, and secure substantial and equal liberty to the people." George Mason began writing.

On June 12, 1776, the convention unanimously adopted Mason's Virginia Declaration of Rights, which began by asserting, "That all men are by nature equally free and independent, and have certain inherent rights, of which, when they enter into

Many people today know little about him, but George Mason was one of America's most influential Founding Fathers. Not only was he the author of Virginia's Declaration of Rights—the document that inspired Thomas Jefferson as he drafted America's Declaration of Independence— he was largely responsible for the addition of the Bill of Rights to the U.S. Constitution.

Author of Virginia's Declaration of Rights (left), George Mason played an active role in drafting the Constitution at the Constitutional Convention in May 1787 (above). But in the end he refused to sign the document. He objected because it lacked a bill of rights and because it allowed the slave trade to continue.

VIRGINIA BILL of RIGHTS

DRAWN ORIGINALLY BY GEORGE MASON AND
ADOPTED BY THE CONVENTION OF DELEGATES

June 12, 1776.

A Declaration of Rights made by the Reprefentatives of the good People of Virginia, affembled in full and free Convention; which Rights do pertain to them, and their Pofterity, as the Bafis and Foundation of Government.

I.

That all Men are by Nature equally free and independent, and have certain inherent Rights, of which, when they enter into a State of Society, they cannot, by any Compact, deprive or divest their Posterity; namely, the Enjoyment of Life and Liberty, with the Means of acquiring and possessing Property, and pursuing and obtaining Happiness and Safety.

II.

That all Power is vested in, and consequently derived from, the People; that Magistrates are their Trustees and Servants, and at all Times amenable to them.

III.

That Government is, or ought to be, instituted for the common Benefit, Protection, and Security, of the People, Nation, or Community; of all the various Modes and Forms of Government that is best, which is capable of producing the greatest Degree of Happiness and Safety, and is most effectually secured against the Danger of Mal-administration; and that, whenever any Government shall be found inadequate or contrary to these Purposes, a Majority of the Community

hath an indubitable, unalienable, and indefeasible Right, to reform, alter, or abolish it, in such Manner as shall be judged most conducive to the public Weal.

IV.

That no Man, or Set of Men, are entitled to exclusive or separate Emoluments or Privileges from the Community, but in Consideration of public Services; which, not being descendible, neither ought the Offices of Magistrate, Legislator, or Judge, to be hereditary.

V.

That the legislative and executive Powers of the State should be separate and distinct from the Judicative; and, that the Members of the two first may be restrained from Oppression, by feeling and participating the Burthens of the People, they should, at fixed Periods, be reduced to a private Station, return into that Body from which they were originally taken, and the Vacancies be supplied by frequent, certain, and regular Elections, in which all, or any Part of the former Members, to be again eligible, or ineligible, as the Laws shall direct. That

a state of society, they cannot, by any compact, deprive or divest their posterity, namely, the enjoyment of life and liberty, with the means of acquiring and possessing property, and pursuing and obtaining happiness and safety." It was a groundbreaking document, one of the first formal declarations of basic human rights. It went on to claim that government derives its power from the people, and that when government fails the people they have the right "to reform, alter, or abolish it." Two weeks later the convention adopted Virginia's first state constitution, which was also framed by Mason. It called for separation of the legislative, executive, and judicial branches of government.

The words and ideas in Virginia's Declaration of Rights probably sound familiar. That's because Thomas Jefferson drew inspiration from Mason's work when he drafted the American Declaration of Independence just a few weeks later.

During the Revolutionary War, Mason served in Virginia's House of Burgesses. At war's end he retired from public office. Duty to his new country lured him away from Gunston Hall in 1787, when the Virginia legislature appointed him to serve as a delegate to the Constitutional Convention in Philadelphia. On the eve of the convention, he wrote to his son George: "It is easy to foresee that there will be much Difficulty in organizing a Government upon this great Scale...yet with the proper Degree of Coolness, Liberality, & Candor (very rare Commodities by the Bye), I doubt not but it may be effected."

Mason played a key part in framing the Constitution. At the last moment, however, he was one of three delegates who refused to sign the final draft of the document. He showed no "coolness" about it. According to fellow Virginia delegate James Madison, Mason angrily said "that he would sooner chop off his right hand than put it to the constitution as it now stands."

Mason and the other anti-Federalist delegates believed the new government created in the document was far too complex. His chief objection to the Constitution, however, was that it lacked a bill of rights to protect individual liberties from a powerful federal government. "The security of our liberty and happiness is the object we ought to have in view in wishing to establish the union," he said. "If instead of securing these, we endanger them, the name of the union will be but a trivial consolation."

He also opposed the provision in the Constitution that allowed the slave trade to continue for another 20 years. He foresaw the trouble it would cause the young nation: "As much as I value an union of all the states, I would not admit the southern states into the union, unless they agreed to the discontinuance of this disgraceful trade, because it would bring weakness and not strength to the union." Ironically, Mason was one of the largest slaveowners in the country. His reliance on the income he earned from slave labor apparently outweighed his contempt for the "slow poison" of slavery.

Mason's stand against the Constitution soured his friendship with George Washington and others, but he had no regrets. "I am truly conscious of having acted from the purest motives of honesty, and love to my country," he wrote to his son John.

Although Mason's demand for a bill of rights failed, his arguments inspired others to take up the cause. In December 1791, the first ten amendments, known as the Bill of Rights, were added to the Constitution. Many of the amendments echoed the ideals Mason had established in the Virginia Declaration of Rights, including freedom of religion, freedom of speech, and the right to a speedy and public trial.

Mason died at Gunston Hall the following year.

> "That the freedom of the press is one of the great bulwarks of liberty, and can never be restrained but by despotic governments."
>
> Virginia Declaration of Rights, June 12, 1776

Lewis and Clark

MERIWETHER LEWIS

BORN   August 18, 1774, near
Charlottesville, Virginia

DIED   October 11, 1809, near
Nashville, Tennessee

AGE AT DEATH   35

FAMILY   Lewis was the son of William
and Lucy Meriwether Lewis.

WILLIAM CLARK

BORN   August 1, 1770, Caroline County,
Virginia

DIED   September 1, 1838, St. Louis,
Missouri

AGE AT DEATH   68

FAMILY   Clark's older brother was a
general in the Revolutionary
War. Clark was married twice
and had seven children.

LANDMARKS   Lewis and Clark National
Historic Trail, which makes
its way through 11 states

MILESTONES   January 18, 1803: Congress
approves funding for the
expedition. September 23,
1806: Successful expedition
returns to St. Louis, Missouri.

Did You Know?

- Thomas Jefferson taught Lewis how to navigate by sextant.
- To show their friendly intentions, the Corps of Discovery gave the Native Americans they met in their travels calico shirts, beads, and fishhooks.
- The expedition noted some 80 plants and 122 animals they had never seen before.
- Lewis and Clark kept expedition journals, and wrote more than a million words.
- Lewis died before the notes from the expedition were published in 1814.
- Throughout the grueling journey, there is no hint that Lewis and Clark argued.

On June 19, 1803, Captain Meriwether Lewis picked up a quill and wrote a letter to his friend William Clark. He said that President Thomas Jefferson wished him to lead a military expedition to explore "those western rivers which may run all the way across North America to the western ocean," with the aim of beginning trade with Indian tribes, discovering new plants and animals, and making maps. Lewis asked Clark, "If therefore there is anything...which would induce you to participate with me in [this enterprise's] fatigues, its dangers, and its honors...Pray write to me on this subject as early as possible...."

A month later, Clark replied: "Dear Lewis, I received by yesterday's mail your letter...The Contents of which I read with much pleasure. I will cheerfully join you...I shall arrange my matters as well as I can against your arrival here." Thus began the partnership of Lewis and Clark, who would soon embark on one of the most famous expeditions in American history.

Meriwether Lewis had known Thomas Jefferson all his life. The son of a Revolutionary War officer, he was born close to Monticello, Jefferson's home in Charlottesville, Virginia. His father died when he was five years old, and Jefferson took an interest in the boy. Jefferson later recalled that Lewis "was remarkable even in infancy for enterprise, boldness and discretion. When only 8 years of age, he habitually went out in the dead of night alone with his dogs, into the forest to hunt the raccoon and opossum."

Lewis inherited his father's plantation, but farming life didn't appeal to him. He hankered for adventure.

As captains Meriwether Lewis and William Clark and their men pushed west to the Pacific Ocean, they ran into dangerous rapids (left)—just one of the many perils they faced on their legendary journey into uncharted lands. The men returned as heroes, and their achievements have been honored ever since, as in the postage stamp above.

Captain William Clark (below left) was the expedition's main cartographer and artist. Both he and Lewis made scientific observations and recorded details of what they saw in their journals (above). They also collected specimens of animals and plants to take back to their curious President.

When he was 20 he asked his mother to oversee the plantation and the slaves who labored there, and he joined the army. He served for six years in the Northwest Territory, where he was exposed to American Indian cultures and languages—which proved useful experience for later.

Soon after Jefferson became President in 1801, he asked Lewis to be his private secretary. He had a special job in mind for his fellow Virginian: He wanted Lewis to lead a group of explorers across the American continent to the Pacific Ocean. Over the next two years,

Jefferson, aided by his friends in the natural sciences, prepared Lewis for the mission. Lewis had gone to school for less than five years, but he quickly absorbed lessons in navigation, surveying, mapmaking, astronomy, botany, and zoology. He even received a crash course in practicing medicine.

In May 1803 the United States bought the vast Louisiana Territory from France for about $15 million—about four cents an acre. The purchase doubled the size of the young nation. The expedition Lewis had been preparing for took on new significance. President Jefferson and Congress were eager to know just what America now owned.

Lewis chose William Clark to help him lead the expedition. Several years earlier he had

"Great joy in camp. We are in View of the Ocean, this great Pacific Ocean which we have been So long anxious to See."

William Clark, November 7, 1805

When President Thomas Jefferson offered Captain Meriwether Lewis (below right) leadership of an expedition to the Pacific Ocean in 1803, Lewis leaped at the chance for adventure. The explorers covered almost 8,000 miles of uncharted wilderness on their trip to the west coast and back (above).

served under Clark in the Army for six months. That was enough time for the two men to size each other up and develop a strong mutual trust.

Born in Caroline County, Virginia, Clark was four years older than Lewis. When Clark was 14 his family moved to the Kentucky frontier. When he was 19 years old he joined the frontier militia and fought against Native Americans who had been attacking settlers in the Ohio Valley. A few years later he signed up with the Army and took command of a special company of sharpshooters. That's when he met Lewis. Later on Clark worked in military intelligence. In 1796 he retired to manage his family's affairs in Kentucky.

Although he had less schooling than Lewis,

Clark brought his own strengths to the partnership. He knew how to deal with Indians, and when necessary, fight them. He was a skilled waterman, surveyor, and mapmaker. He shared Lewis's love of the wilderness and of open spaces—and his curiosity. So when Lewis's letter reached him, Clark jumped at the opportunity to blaze new trails with his good friend.

Captain Lewis and Captain Clark recruited about 40 men, including Clark's slave, York, for the Corps of Discovery. In May 1804 the expedition set out from St. Louis and started

"We were now about to penetrate a country at least two thousand miles in width, on which the foot of civilized man had never trodden."

Meriwether Lewis, April 7, 1805

Among the members of the expedition was an African-American slave named York, who was owned by William Clark. Many of the Indians the explorers encountered had never seen a black man before. As shown in this painting, the chief of one tribe, finding it hard to believe that a man's skin could be so dark, tried to rub the color off York's chest.

working its way up the Missouri River in a 55-foot keelboat and two smaller boats. It was rough going. The company fought against the current all the way, hauling a heavy cargo of supplies, including guns and ammunition, ink and paper, food, clothing, whiskey and tobacco, and 21 bales of beads, trinkets, and other gifts to trade with Indians.

Along the way the explorers made maps and kept detailed journals of what they saw. They also made contact with several Native American tribes. Lewis and Clark gave the Indians presents and encouraged their leaders to "obey the commands of their great Chief the President [Jefferson] who is now your only great father." Most of the encounters were friendly, although there were some tense moments.

In October the company reached what is now North Dakota. They built a fort near a friendly Mandan and Hidatsa Indian village along the Missouri's banks and settled in for the winter. One day a French-Canadian fur trader named Toussaint Charbonneau showed up at the

fort, seeking a job as a guide and interpreter. He was accompanied by his teenage wife, Sacagawea *(pages 50–51)* of the Shoshone tribe, which lived near the Rocky Mountains. The captains hoped she could help them bargain with her people for horses to take them over the peaks.

In the spring of 1805, Lewis and Clark sent a small crew back to St. Louis with the keelboat. The crew took with them a detailed report to Jefferson about what the explorers had seen and learned so far, as well as maps drawn by Clark. They also took "a number of articles to the President of the United States," including animal skins and skeletons, plants and seeds, soil and rock samples, a live prairie dog, and several live birds.

Lewis and Clark and the rest of the Corps of Discovery, now accompanied by Charbonneau, Sacagawea, and their newborn son, continued up the Missouri River in canoes. They had no idea what lay between them and the Pacific Ocean, but they were determined to keep heading west until they reached the sea. Along the way they passed through vast grasslands and saw "immense herds of Buffalo, Elk, deer & Antelopes feeding in one common and boundless pasture." They discovered animals new to them, including the gray wolf, the sage grouse, and the grizzly bear, whose strength and ferocity astonished and alarmed them.

As the expedition pressed westward, the river developed dangerous rapids and waterfalls. At one point they abandoned the water, carrying their canoes and cargo for 16 back-breaking miles. At last they reached the Rockies. Sacagawea helped guide them to the Shoshone, who traded a number of horses to the white men.

It took the explorers 11 days to cross the rugged mountains, and they nearly starved and froze on the way. On the other side they met friendly Nez Perce Indians, who helped them make canoes for the final part of their journey.

Traveling down the Clearwater, Snake, and Columbia Rivers, Captains Lewis and Clark and their comrades rejoiced when they finally reached the Pacific Ocean in November 1805. They built a fort near the coast, where they endured the harsh winter with the help of local Chinook and Clatsop Indians.

In March 1806 the Corps of Discovery started their homeward trek. At Fort Mandan they bid farewell to Sacagawea and her husband and child. In September they reached St. Louis, where they were welcomed as heroes by cheering citizens.

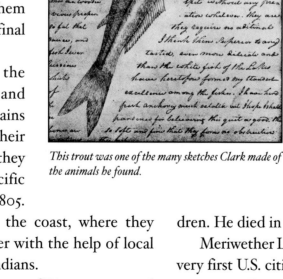

This trout was one of the many sketches Clark made of the animals he found.

Lewis and Clark's detailed journals and maps, their accounts of the Native Americans they encountered, and the thousands of specimens they brought back from their travels excited curiosity throughout the country. Lewis reported to President Jefferson that unfortunately there was no all-water route linking the Atlantic and Pacific Oceans, but that the new U.S. territory teemed with game and lands for farming. The news sent thousands of Americans heading west.

To reward Lewis for his service to the nation, Jefferson appointed him governor of the Louisiana Territory. Lewis was never very happy in the job, however. In 1809 he committed suicide. Historians today believe that he suffered from depression.

Clark fared much better. Jefferson appointed him brigadier general of the militia and superintendent of Indian affairs for the Louisiana Territory. Later on Clark served as governor of the Missouri Territory for several years. He married twice and had seven children. He died in 1838 at the age of 68.

Meriwether Lewis and William Clark were the very first U.S. citizens ever to cross the American continent. During their trip to the Pacific and back, they covered almost 8,000 miles of wilderness. Today the brave adventurers still excite admiration for boldly going into uncharted lands and blazing a path for others to follow.

Sacagawea

BORN	circa 1786, probably near present-day Lemhi, Idaho
DIED	circa December 20, 1812, Fort Manuel, on the Missouri River, Dakota Territory
AGE AT DEATH	26?
OTHER NAMES	Sacagawea (Sah-ka-gah-WEE-uh) means "bird woman." William Clark called her Janey. Boinaiv, her Shoshone name, means "grass maiden."
FAMILY	Son: Jean-Baptiste, with husband Toussaint Charbonneau, a fur trapper. Daughter: Lisette, presumably died young.
LANDMARKS	Statue in Washington Park, Portland, Oregon

Did You Know?

- Sacagawea was from the Lemhi band of Shoshone Indians.
- William Clark became the guardian of Sacagawea's son, Jean-Baptiste. He was very fond of the boy and nicknamed him Pomp. Pomp later traveled to Europe with a prince and was also a guide and administrator at San Luis Rey Mission in California.
- When the expedition finally reached the Pacific, in a rare demand Sacagawea insisted on going to the shore to see the "great waters" and the "monstrous fish"—a beached whale.
- Very little is known about her life, and the year of her death is unclear. Some Native American oral traditions suggest that Sacagawea lived to ripe old age.
- In 2000 the United States put her likeness on the dollar coin, which replaced the Susan B. Anthony dollar coin.
- More monuments, memorials, rivers, lakes, and mountain areas are said to have been named for Sacagawea than for any other American woman.

WHEN CAPTAINS Meriwether Lewis and William Clark *(pages 44–49)* led their famous expedition in the early 1800s, they took with them an American Indian teenager called Sacagawea.

Born into the Shoshone tribe in what is now Idaho, Sacagawea became a war captive of Hidatsa Indians in North Dakota when she was about ten years old. That was where she met Lewis and Clark, who were wintering there before pushing west. By this time Sacagawea was about 15 and had been most likely sold in marriage to a French-Canadian fur trapper named Toussaint Charbonneau. The captains hired him as an interpreter, thinking his Shoshone wife might help them negotiate with her people.

In spring 1805 the expedition headed west on the Missouri River with Sacagawea and her two-month-old son, Jean-Baptiste. She soon proved a valuable member of the team. She collected roots, berries, and other plants to help feed the men. When a boat tipped over during a squall, she gathered up the captains' journals and other items to keep them from drifting away.

Eventually the explorers met the Shoshone. Sacagawea's brother had become chief, and she persuaded him to trade horses to the team so they could cross the Rocky Mountains. Along the way, they met many other tribes. Sacagawea's presence showed the company was peaceful, because as Clark wrote, "A woman with a party of men is a token of peace."

After the expedition Sacagawea went back to North Dakota, where she is believed to have died in 1812, at about age 26. Over the years, the few known facts about her life have blended with myth, making her one of the most famous figures in American history.

This statue of Sacagawea and her infant son stands in the Rotunda of the U.S. Capitol. Popular legend holds that Sacagawea showed the Lewis and Clark expedition the way west, as suggested in the painting at left, but scholars believe her role as a guide has been exaggerated. Nonetheless she was a courageous and valuable member of the expedition.

Tecumseh

Did You Know?

- Tecumseh believed that if the British won the War of 1812, their settlement with Native Americans would be more favorable than one with the United States.
- Tecumseh believed that no one could own the air, sky, and land—and that these resources belonged to everyone.
- Tecumseh and his brother founded Prophetstown in Indiana, near Tippecanoe Creek. After a battle with William Henry Harrison in November 1811, the settlement was abandoned. This earned Harrison the nickname "Tippecanoe."
- Tecumseh was well known for his eloquence. In September 1813, he gave a speech to Major General Henry Procter, the British commander of Fort Malden, and declared, "Our lives are in the hands of the Great Spirit. We are determined to defend our lands, and if it be His will, we wish to leave our bones upon them."

In the early 1800s, a young Shawnee chief from the Ohio River Valley came up with a bold plan. The best way to stop the persistent westward movement of white settlers, Tecumseh decided, was to unite the continent's various Indian tribes into one great nation.

A magnetic leader and brilliant organizer, Tecumseh visited tribes from the Great Lakes to the Gulf of Mexico to urge them to unite. His brother Tenskwatawa, a religious leader known as the Prophet, often went with him. The Prophet called on the tribes to reject white customs and return to traditional Indian ways. Tecumseh pointed out that even though the tribes had many differences, they all faced a common threat. An Indian confederacy, he said, would be strong enough to keep the United States from spreading farther west. He also spoke out against the land deals some Indian chiefs were making with the whites. He argued that no single tribe owned the land, so it wasn't theirs to sell. His ideas won over many young warriors, who—like Tecumseh—were ready to fight to the death to preserve the American Indian way of life.

Alarmed by the ever increasing number of braves joining Tecumseh's alliance, future President William Henry Harrison, governor of the Indiana Territory, attempted negotiations with Tecumseh. In their meeting, the warrior scoffed at the idea that land could be sold: "Sell a country! Why not sell the air, the clouds and the great sea, as well as the earth?"

When the War of 1812 broke out, Tecumseh and his followers sided with the British and fought fiercely against the Americans. In 1813 Tecumseh was killed in battle. Without his leadership, the tribal confederacy fell apart. Today Tecumseh is remembered for his vision of Indian unity and his determined defense of his people's native lands.

Tecumseh refused to cooperate when the United States tried to negotiate for Indian lands. "These lands are ours" he declared. "No one has a right to remove us, because we were the first owners....As to boundaries, the Great Spirit knows no boundaries, nor will his red children acknowledge any."

John Chapman

BORN	September 26, 1774, Leominster, Massachusetts
DIED	circa March 18, 1845, near Fort Wayne, Indiana
AGE AT DEATH	71
OTHER NAMES	Johnny Appleseed
FAMILY	Father: Nathaniel Chapman, a carpenter. Mother: Elizabeth Symond Chapman, died of tuberculosis when he was only two years old. He had a stepmother, Lucy Cooley, and ten half siblings.
HONORS	1996: Chapman was designated the official folk hero of the Commonwealth of Massachusetts.

Did You Know?

- Chapman's father was a minuteman at Concord.
- Planting an apple orchard served as a way of claiming a parcel of land.
- Chapman collected his apple seeds from cider presses. He wore a sack or a shirt, and was fond of walking barefoot. Although he is usually pictured wearing an inverted mush pan for a hat, there's no evidence that he did—that's part of the myth that's grown up around him.
- As he traveled the frontier, he slept outdoors or sheltered overnight with pioneer families. He also would preach sermons on the spur of the moment.
- Chapman's faith was important to him, and one way he practiced his beliefs was by being kind to people and animals.
- At the time of his death he owned more than a thousand acres of land.

Some frontiersmen, such as Daniel Boone and Davy Crockett, made names for themselves with their hunting and fighting skills. John Chapman earned his place in history by gentler means: He planted apple trees.

Better known as Johnny Appleseed, Chapman was born in 1774 in Leominster, Massachusetts. Little is known of his early years. At age 23 or so he made his way to the wilds of northwestern Pennsylvania, where he planted the seeds for his first apple tree nursery. He sold his seedlings to settlers moving into the region.

Around 1800 Chapman headed west into frontier territory, laden with burlap bags of apple seeds he had collected from cider presses. He had a knack for judging where pioneers would be likely to settle, and he planted his nurseries there. By the time the homesteaders arrived, Chapman had apple seedlings ready for them to start their own orchards. If people couldn't afford to buy the seedlings, he traded them for food or just gave them away.

For nearly half a century, Chapman roamed what would become Ohio and Indiana, tending his nurseries and planting new ones. He earned enough cash to buy more than a thousand acres, yet he dressed in ragged clothes and often went barefoot.

Chapman became a legend in his own time, known for his eccentric appearance, his generosity, his wilderness skills, his friendship with Native Americans, his knowledge of the Bible, and of course his apples, which were a mainstay of the pioneer diet. His mythic image grew when he risked his life to warn settlers of Indian attacks during the War of 1812. Chapman died of pneumonia in 1845. He lives on as one of America's favorite folk heroes: Johnny Appleseed.

John Chapman, better known as Johnny Appleseed, is celebrated in songs, folk tales, books, poems, postage stamps (above), and even a Disney film. His life has become so intertwined with legend that it's hard to tell what is fact about him and what is fiction. What we do know is that he won his fame by planting apple trees.

A NEW BIRTH OF FREEDOM

Civil War and Reconstruction

★ 1848–1877 ★

By the mid-1840s, the northern and southern states were taking different economic paths. The economy of the North increasingly focused on industry and commerce, while the agricultural economy of the South depended heavily on slave labor. The debate over slavery started to drive a wedge between the North and the South. In the meantime, hundreds of thousands of pioneers migrated west to

1848

People from across the country and around the world flocked to California after gold was discovered there in 1848. Prospectors (above) sifted flakes of gold from streambeds.

1861–1865

The four-year Civil War claimed more than half a million American lives. The Confederate loss at Gettysburg in 1863 (above) was a turning point in the war. That battle alone saw some 50,000 dead.

1867

The United States bought Alaska from Russia for about two cents an acre in 1867. Formerly a Russian fur-trading center, Sitka (above) was the first capital of the vast territory.

1869

The joining of the tracks of the Central Pacific and the Union Pacific lines at Promontory, Utah, in 1869 was cause for champagne celebration. It created America's first transcontinental railroad.

claim free or cheap government land. In 1848 the discovery of gold at Sutter's Mill in California gave the country a case of gold fever. Thousands of people stampeded to the foothills of California's Sierra Nevada to make their fortune. Some of the prospectors became enormously wealthy; most did not.

The other momentous event of 1848 took place in a small town in upstate New York called Seneca Falls. That July, more than 200 women (and 40 men) gathered there for a convention to "discuss the social, civil and religious condition and rights of Woman." A third of those in attendance signed a declaration that called for equality for women in education, law, labor, morality, and

★

*"The right [to vote] is ours.
Have it, we must. Use it, we will."*

Elizabeth Cady Stanton, Seneca Falls Convention,
July 19, 1848

★

religion. The boldest demand was for a woman's right to vote—a right that wasn't even considered when the Founding Fathers framed the Constitution.

Many of the people who supported women's rights were also abolitionists—people who believed that slavery was evil and should be abolished. Some of the most courageous abolitionists were former slaves who put their lives on the line for freedom. In 1861 the slavery issue erupted into a bloody civil war when the southern states seceded from the Union. In the period following the war, known as Reconstruction, black and white citizens began the work of transforming the South and putting the nation back together again.

Sojourner Truth

Did You Know?

- As a young girl Sojourner Truth was bought by a slave owner named John Dumont. She had five children with the slave Dumont chose to be her husband, but many were sold to different owners. Sojourner later sued Dumont because he had illegally sold her child, Peter, to a slave owner outside of the state. She was the first black woman to sue a white man in court. She won the case.

- In 1850, Sojourner Truth published her autobiography, *Narrative of Sojourner Truth*. It was ghostwritten, since she did not know how to write. She sold copies for 25 cents and lived off the proceeds.

- In the 1860s Sojourner Truth filed and won a lawsuit that stated that black people had the right to ride on public transportation just as white people did.

- During the Civil War, she gathered supplies for black Union soldiers.

- After the war she worked on a plan to resettle former slaves in the West.

THE CHARISMATIC BLACK abolitionist leader Sojourner Truth knew firsthand about the evils of slavery. She lived her first 30 years as a slave. Born Isabella Baumfree, she grew up in upstate New York, where she was owned by several masters and beaten by some of them. Shortly before slavery was banned by the state in 1827, she escaped from her owner.

Baumfree moved to New York City, where she worked as a house servant. In 1843 she had a vision that called for her to sojourn, or journey, across the land as a preacher. She renamed herself Sojourner Truth. "The Lord gave me Truth," she said, "because I was to declare truth unto people."

In the following years, Truth traveled through the Northeast and the Midwest. Tall and strong, with a deep, rumbling voice, she preached at churches, camp meetings, and on village streets. She spoke of divine love and the brotherhood of man, and she railed against slavery. As Truth's reputation as a powerful orator grew, large crowds gathered to hear her. Her words inspired many to take up the cause of abolition.

Truth also spoke out for women's rights. Her speech at a women's rights convention in Ohio in 1851 electrified the audience. She demanded that poor and working women be given their due and used herself as an example: "I could work as much and eat as much as a man—when I could get it—and bear the lash as well! And ain't I a woman?"

In 1864 she met with President Lincoln at the White House to discuss how to help freed slaves. In 1875 Truth finally gave up her sojourning and settled down in Michigan.

When Sojourner Truth preached, she electrified her audiences with her strong belief in God's goodness and her passionate opposition to slavery. Her words inspired many people to join the abolitionist movement. Truth supported herself by selling copies of her autobiography (above).

Harriet Tubman

BORN	circa 1820, Dorchester County, Maryland
DIED	March 10, 1913, Auburn, New York
AGE AT DEATH	93?
OTHER NAMES	Araminta Ross (birth name). She later adopted her mother's name, Harriet. She was called "The Moses of Her People."
FAMILY	Married John Tubman, a free African American, in 1844. Married Nelson Davis in 1869. Tubman had no children.
LANDMARKS	Harriet Tubman Home, Auburn, New York
HONORS	1944: Eleanor Roosevelt christened the liberty ship, S.S. *Harriet Tubman*. 1978: A postage stamp was issued in her honor.

Did You Know?

- While the Fugitive Slave Act of 1850 made it illegal to help runaway slaves, neither Tubman, nor any of the people she helped escape from slavery, were ever caught.
- It is possible Tubman suffered from narcolepsy, an illness which causes unexpected bouts of deep sleep. Her head injury as a teenager may have been the cause.
- Tubman made at least 19 trips herself on the Underground Railroad.
- Sometimes, if Tubman was being chased while leading slaves to freedom, she would head them back South to confuse her pursuers.
- Harriet tried for years to get the government to pay her a pension for her Civil War services. She received a small pension starting in 1890.
- The Harriet Tubman Family Living Center in New York City offers shelter to the homeless.

IN THE YEARS BEFORE THE CIVIL WAR, thousands of slaves made their way to freedom along escape routes that became known as the Underground Railroad. One of the most daring conductors, or guides, on the Railroad was an ex-slave named Harriet Tubman. She helped lead so many blacks to freedom that she became known as Moses, after the biblical leader who led the Hebrews out of bondage in Egypt.

Harriet Tubman was born on a Maryland plantation around 1820. She began to work as a house slave at age five, and at thirteen she was put to work in the fields. Like many slaves, she was underfed and overworked, but her spirit stayed strong. When Harriet was in her early teens, she tried to protect another slave from a beating by the overseer. In the confusion he struck her in the head with a two-pound weight, which knocked her unconscious. As a result of the blow, she suffered from blackouts and seizures the rest of her life.

After Harriet recovered, her owner put her back to work driving oxen, chopping wood, and plowing fields. She didn't mind the heavy physical labor, since she preferred to be outdoors. At about age 25, she married a free black man named John Tubman. Harriet longed to be free herself, and in 1849 she decided to run away after learning that she and some other slaves on the plantation might be sold. Leaving her husband behind, she followed the North Star by night and hid by day. After walking a hundred miles, she reached Pennsylvania—and sweet liberty. Once there, she recalled, "I looked at my hands to see if I was the same person now I was free."

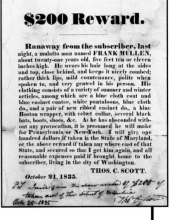

The most famous conductor on the Underground Railroad, Harriet Tubman risked her life again and again to lead some 300 slaves out of bondage in the South to freedom in Canada. Bounty hunters tracked down runaways to collect rewards offered for their capture (above). Eventually Harriet had a price of $40,000 on her head.

Harriet Tubman, far left, poses with a group of former slaves she helped escape. Among the indignities runaways left behind them was being forced to wear an identity tag (below). Slaves found without tags or other identification were jailed.

Tubman settled in Philadelphia, where she found work as a servant. She gloried in her freedom, even as she planned to risk it by returning to the South to rescue her family members. William Still, the Philadelphia Stationmaster of the Underground Railroad, befriended Harriet. From him she learned all about the secret network of individuals—many of them Quakers—who assisted runaway blacks and provided safe places for them to hide from slave catchers.

In 1851 Tubman slipped back into Maryland to rescue her sister and her sister's children and take them to the North. That was the beginning of her career as an Underground Railroad conductor. Over the next ten years she made the dangerous journey back to the South another 18 times and guided some 300 slaves, including her elderly parents and several of her brothers and sisters, to freedom in Canada. (John Tubman, who had taken another wife, chose to stay behind.)

Coolheaded and courageous, Harriet conducted her passengers North in the cold winter months, when people stayed indoors and darkness came early. The groups usually traveled by night, along routes that Harriet had carefully planned in advance. They mostly walked but sometimes went by horse and cart, boat, or train. During the day the runaways hid in swamps, forests, and safe houses.

Harriet used a variety of tricks—including

disguises and forged papers—to outwit the bounty hunters. Like a military commander, she demanded complete obedience from her followers. She knew that one false move could result in capture, and she was determined not to let that happen. She drugged babies to keep them from making noise during an escape. And she had no patience with runaways who started talking about turning back because they were tired or frightened. She reminded them that a live runaway could do great harm by going back, but that a dead one could tell no secrets. Gesturing with the gun she always carried, she gave them a choice: "Go on or die." They all chose freedom.

As she later pointed out with pride, Tubman "never lost a single passenger" in all her trips. Indeed, so successful was she at smuggling slaves that slave owners eventually put a $40,000 reward on her head. To abolitionists, however, Tubman was a hero, and she became acquainted with such antislavery leaders as Frederick Douglass *(see pages 72–75)* and Sojourner Truth *(see pages 58–59)*.

During the Civil War, Tubman served the Union Army as a nurse, cook, and spy. Fearless as ever, she stole across Confederate lines and scouted out warehouses, ammunition depots, and other military sites.

After the war Tubman settled with her elderly parents on a small farm near Auburn, New York, and she married a black veteran named Nelson Davis. Keeping the name Tubman, she continued to work to improve the lives of African Americans. She supported schooling for free blacks, and she later transformed her farm into a shelter for poor and aged African Americans. She also campaigned for women's voting rights. Harriet Tubman died in 1913 and was buried with military honors in recognition of her contributions to her country.

> "When I found
> that I had crossed that line,
> I looked at my hands to see
> if I was the same person
> now I was free.
> There was such a glory
> over everything...
> I felt like I was in heaven."

To her biographer, published 1869

If any of Tubman's "passengers" had second thoughts and wanted to turn back, she threatened them with the gun she always carried. "Go on or die," she warned.

Abraham Lincoln

BORN February 12, 1809, near Hodgenville, Kentucky

DIED April 15, 1865, in Washington, D.C.; assassinated by John Wilkes Booth

AGE AT DEATH 56

OTHER NAMES Honest Abe, the Great Emancipator

FAMILY Lincoln's mother died when he was nine years old. He called his stepmother his "angel mother." Lincoln and his wife, Mary Todd Lincoln, had four children—all boys—Robert, Edward, William, Thomas. Edward died in childhood and William died of typhoid fever.

LANDMARKS Springfield, Illinois (home and grave). Lincoln Memorial, Washington, D.C.

MILESTONES March 4, 1861–April 15, 1865: 16th President of the United States. January 1, 1863: Emancipation Proclamation, which promised to free slaves in states that had seceded from the Union

Did You Know?

- At six feet, four inches tall, Lincoln was the tallest President.
- Lincoln established the Department of Agriculture and opened up federal land to settlers.
- Some of Lincoln's favorite books were *Aesop's Fables* and *Robinson Crusoe*. He also enjoyed history and works by Shakespeare.
- During his lifetime, Lincoln also worked as a blacksmith and as a lobbyist for Illinois Central Railroad.

ABRAHAM LINCOLN LED OUR NATION through its greatest crisis—civil war. His determination to save the Union and end slavery made him one of America's greatest national heroes.

Born in a log cabin in Kentucky, Lincoln grew up helping his family scratch out a living from the land. Neither of his parents could read or write. Lincoln himself was able to attend school for only a few weeks or months at a time, when he could be spared from his chores at home. But he hungered for knowledge, and he educated himself by reading borrowed books and newspapers.

When Lincoln was 21, his family moved to Illinois. There he worked as a rail splitter, a flatboat navigator, a storekeeper, a post-master, and a soldier in the Army. At the age of 25 he was elected to the Illinois Legislature. He taught himself law, passed the exams, and accepted a job as a junior partner in a law firm in Springfield, the new capital of Illinois. In 1842 Lincoln married Mary Todd.

Lincoln went on to serve a term in the U.S. House of Representatives, where he spoke out against the spread of slavery, which he called a "monstrous injustice." He twice ran for the U.S. Senate in the 1850s and lost. However, the debates he had about slavery with his 1858 Senate opponent, Stephen Douglas, gained Lincoln a national reputation and helped him win the presidential race of 1860.

Running as a Republican, Lincoln promised to end the spread of slavery into American territories, although he did not propose to end slavery itself. He also said that he considered it treason for southern states to secede, or withdraw, from the Union.

The photograph at left, taken four days before his assassination, reveals the strain the Civil War put on Abraham Lincoln. Unlike George Washington, America's other great national hero, Lincoln was born into humble circumstances. Before he entered politics, he worked as a flatboat navigator, storekeeper, postmaster, and rail splitter (above).

Early in the Civil War, Lincoln (center) appointed George B. McClellan (sixth from left) head of the Union Army. When McClellan proved indecisive and overcautious, Lincoln dismissed him in favor of another general. In 1864 Lincoln gave the command to Ulysses S. Grant, whose bold approach helped wrap up the war.

Six weeks after Lincoln's victory, South Carolina acted on its threat to secede rather than accept the Republican plan. Six more slave states seceded soon afterward. In February 1861 these seven states combined to form the Confederate States of America. Despite this action, Lincoln hoped to find a way to preserve the Union peacefully. But these hopes ended on April 12, 1861, when Confederate forces opened fire on Fort Sumter, a U.S. garrison in the harbor of Charleston, South Carolina. The Civil War, the bloodiest conflict in American history, had begun.

In his Inaugural Address Lincoln had warned the South that he was sworn to "preserve, protect and defend" the Union. Now he took steps to do so. Without consulting Congress, which was out of session at the time, he expanded the size of

In the Emancipation Proclamation, issued on January 1, 1863, Lincoln formally committed the U.S. government to freeing slaves.

the Army and Navy. He ordered a blockade of Confederate ports to keep foreign nations from sending weapons to the South. And he competed with Confederate leaders for the loyalty of states not yet committed to either side. (In the end, 11 states joined the Confederacy, and 23 stayed in the Union.) Extending presidential power to an unprecedented degree, Lincoln also suspended the writ of habeas corpus—the constitutional right that protects people from being jailed without due process of law. He argued that this was justified: "Often limb must be amputated to save a life."

Lincoln made it clear from the start of the war that he fought to save the Union, not to destroy slavery. In August 1862 he wrote, "If I could save the Union without freeing any slave I would do it; and if I could save it by freeing all the slaves I would do it." As the war dragged on, however, he changed his position. This was partly in response to the growth of anti-slavery sentiment in the North, and partly because he concluded that freeing slaves would weaken the Confederacy.

On January 1, 1863, Lincoln issued the Emancipation Proclamation. This famous decree called for an end to slavery in states fighting the Union. To make emancipation official, he encouraged Congress to pass the 13th Amendment, which outlawed slavery everywhere in the nation.

The Union Army's victory at the Battle of Gettysburg, Pennsylvania, in July 1863, marked the turning point in the war. Four months after the battle, Lincoln dedicated the battlefield cemetery. In his famous Gettysburg Address, he inspired Union citizens to keep up the struggle

> "With malice toward none, with charity for all... let us strive on to finish the work we are in, to bind up the nation's wounds...."
>
> Second Inaugural Address, March 4, 1865

so "that these dead shall not have died in vain—that this nation, under God, shall have a new birth of freedom."

Lincoln won reelection in 1864. In his second Inaugural Address, he spoke of his desire for peace. But he warned that the Union would continue to fight "until every drop of blood drawn with the lash shall be paid by another drawn with the sword."

On April 9, 1865, the Confederates finally surrendered at Appomattox Courthouse, Virginia. But Lincoln had little time to savor the victory. On April 14, 1865, Abraham Lincoln was shot by a Confederate sympathizer named John Wilkes Booth. He died the following morning. Millions of Americans mourned the courageous leader who had reunited a divided nation and brought freedom for African Americans.

Abraham Lincoln's assassination by John Wilkes Booth plunged much of the country into mourning. After lying in state at the U.S. Capitol, his body traveled in this hearse to Illinois for burial.

Clara Barton

BORN	December 25, 1821, North Oxford, Massachusetts
DIED	April 12, 1912, Glen Echo, Maryland
AGE AT DEATH	90
OTHER NAMES	Clarissa Harlowe Barton (birth name), Angel of the Battlefield
FAMILY	Father: Stephen Barton, a representative in the Massachusetts state legislature. Mother: Sarah Stone Barton
LANDMARKS	After retiring from the Red Cross, Barton spent the rest of her life at her home in Glen Echo, Maryland, which is now a national historic site.
MILESTONES	May 21, 1881: American Association of the Red Cross was formed. Barton was elected president at a June meeting

Did You Know?

- Barton was born on Christmas Day. Her siblings were much older, so she didn't have anyone to play with growing up. She took care of one of her brothers when he fell off a barn roof.
- Barton started teaching school when she was 17 years old.
- Barton was also devoted to promoting woman suffrage. She was friends with Susan B. Anthony and other suffrage leaders. She also worked on behalf of disenfranchised blacks.
- Barton wrote an autobiography, *The Story of My Childhood,* and a book about her experience in the Red Cross, *The Red Cross in Peace and War.*
- At the age of 76 she traveled to Cuba to join relief workers in the Spanish-American War.
- Barton later described her work on the battlefield as lying "anywhere between the bullet and the hospital."

KNOWN AS THE "ANGEL OF THE BATTLEFIELD" for her extraordinary devotion to wounded soldiers, Clara Barton was one of America's most beloved Civil War heroes. Her dedication to helping others, however, went beyond her courageous wartime deeds.

A former schoolteacher from Massachusetts, Barton moved to Washington, D.C., in 1854. She took a job as a clerk at the U.S. Patent Office, where she demanded—and received—the same pay as male clerks, a rare thing for a woman in those days.

When the Civil War broke out Barton threw her energies into the Union war effort. As she watched wounded soldiers pour into Washington, she realized that the Army desperately needed medical supplies. She made it her job to get them.

Barton recruited volunteers to help her gather medicine and other vital supplies. Then she pestered government and military authorities until they finally gave her permission to deliver the goods to the front lines. With her bonnet and dark skirt, Barton was an unlikely battleground figure. Ignoring bullets and cannonballs, she risked her life at battle after battle to nurse and comfort suffering soldiers. She cooked for them, fed them, took bullets out of them, and held their hands when they were dying.

Near the end of the war, with the approval of President Lincoln, Barton set up an office to search for missing soldiers. In 1869 she went to Europe, where she became associated with the International Red Cross. Back home she organized the American Red Cross to provide humanitarian aid during wartime and in times of natural disasters, such as earthquakes and floods. She died in 1912 at age 90.

Braving the perils of battle, Clara Barton risked her life throughout the Civil War to help soldiers in need (above). A surgeon she assisted at the bloody Battle of Antietam in 1862 praised her as "the true heroine of the age, the angel of the battlefield." After the war Barton founded the American Red Cross.

Mary Edwards Walker

★

BORN	November 26, 1832, near Oswego, New York
DIED	February 21, 1919, Oswego, New York
AGE AT DEATH	87
FAMILY	Walker had one brother and four sisters. In 1856 Walker married Albert Miller, also a doctor. They set up practice together, but it failed after a few years, as did their marriage.
LANDMARKS	Women in Military Service for America Memorial, Arlington, Virginia
MILESTONES	1855: Graduated from Syracuse Medical School
HONORS	1865: Congressional Medal of Honor. In 1917 it was rescinded along with 910 other medals, due to revised standards. Walker never returned the medal and wore it often. Congress reinstated her medal in 1977. 1982: Walker was honored with a 20-cent stamp.

Did You Know?

- Walker's official title during the Civil War was contract acting assistant surgeon (civilian), U. S. Army.
- When Walker arrived in Richmond, Virginia, as a prisoner during the Civil War, a Confederate captain commented that only a "depraved Yankee nation could produce—A Female Doctor."
- Besides her work as a doctor, Walker also wrote for a magazine, *Sybil*.
- Walker wore pants and men's top hats and coats and was arrested for dressing as a man. She even wore a pair of pants at her wedding.
- Walker was elected president of the National Dress Reform Association in 1866.

DR. MARY EDWARDS WALKER was not only among the first women ever to graduate from medical school in America. She was the only woman ever to receive the Congressional Medal of Honor, the highest military award.

Born in 1832 in Oswego, New York, Walker grew up in a family of abolitionists. Her parents believed that girls should be well educated. They also believed that corsets and other women's garments were unhealthy. Walker agreed. She was among the first to don "bloomers"—trousers worn under a knee-length skirt. Her outfit shocked most people, but she argued that the style allowed "freedom of motion and circulation."

In June 1855 Walker graduated from medical school. When the Civil War broke out in 1861, she headed for Washington, D.C. A fervent Union supporter, she tried to join the Army as a surgeon. The military, however, wasn't ready for a woman doctor. Indeed, many men at the time thought women had no right to practice medicine at all.

Rather than return home, Walker volunteered her service in military hospitals and on battlefields. Her skills earned her recognition, and in 1863 she was finally hired as the first female surgeon in the U.S. Army. Some historians believe Walker may also have spied for the Union. Later in the war she was captured and spent four months in a Confederate prison.

When the war ended, President Andrew Johnson awarded Walker the Medal of Honor for devoting "herself with much patriotic zeal to the sick and wounded soldiers...to the detriment of her own health."

After the war, Mary Edwards Walker wrote and lectured in support of women's voting rights and dress reform, and against tobacco and alcohol. She took to wearing full male attire, to which she proudly pinned her Medal of Honor.

During the Civil War, Dr. Mary Edwards Walker fought sexism and military tradition to become the first female surgeon in the U.S. Army. Later in life she crusaded for women's dress reform. "The greatest sorrows from which women suffer today," she wrote, "are those physical, moral, and mental ones that are caused by their unhygienic manner of dressing!"

Frederick Douglass

BORN	circa February 1818, Tuckahoe, Maryland
DIED	February 20, 1895, Washington, D.C.
AGE AT DEATH	77
OTHER NAMES	Frederick Augustus Washington Bailey (birth name). He took the name Douglass to disguise his identity.
FAMILY	Married Anna Murray, a free black from Baltimore, Maryland. They had five children: Rosetta, Lewis Henry, Frederick Jr., Charles Remond, and Annie. After Anna's death, Douglass married his white secretary, Helen Pitts.
LANDMARKS	Frederick Douglass National Historic Site, Washington, D.C.

Did You Know?

- Around the age of 13, Douglass bought a book, *The Columbian Orator,* to teach himself rhetoric.
- Douglass became an agent in the Underground Railroad, helping escaped slaves make their way to Canada.
- In 1848 Douglass attended the first Woman's Rights Convention in Seneca Falls, New York.
- Douglass's autobiography sold more than 30,000 copies in the United States and Great Britain within five years. He also published a novella, *The Heroic Slave,* in 1852.
- Douglass was nominated for Vice President of the United States and ran on the Equal Rights Party ticket in 1852.
- In 1872, fire destroyed Douglass's home and files in Rochester, New York.
- Two of his sons fought in the Civil War.

IN THE FIRST ISSUE OF HIS ABOLITIONIST NEWSPAPER, the *North Star,* Frederick Douglass urged his black readers to "Remember that we are one, that our cause is one, and that we must help each other, if we would succeed. We...have worn the heavy yoke; we have sighed beneath our bonds, and writhed beneath the bloody lash;—cruel mementoes of our oneness are indelibly marked on our living flesh."

Douglass had personally experienced the indignities he described. He spent the first 20 years of his life as a slave. He devoted the rest of it to the causes of freedom and equal rights.

The son of a black slave woman and an unidentified white man, he was born Frederick Bailey on a plantation on Maryland's Eastern Shore around 1818. When he was eight, he was sent to Baltimore to work for a ship carpenter and his wife. Although slave literacy was against the law, Frederick learned to read and write, reportedly with the help of his owner's wife. Secretly reading discarded newspapers, he devoured stories about the growing antislavery movement, known as abolitionism. He also began attending free black churches, where he was inspired by African American men speaking in public about freedom.

The more Frederick thought about freedom, the more defiant he became. To punish him, when he was about 15 his master hired him out to a farmer with a reputation as a slave breaker. The brutal man whipped Frederick daily, but he couldn't beat out the teenager's dream of freedom. In 1836 Frederick's owner sent

Famous abolitionist Frederick Douglass stirred the conscience of the North with his eloquent speeches (above), books, and articles. He believed that forceful action, perhaps even violence, was needed to end slavery. In an 1857 speech he compared, "those who profess to favor freedom and yet deprecate agitation" with "men who want crops without plowing up the ground."

> "What, to the American slave, is your Fourth of July?
> I answer: A day that reveals to him, more than all other days in the year,
> the gross injustice and cruelty to which he is the constant victim.
> To him, your celebration is a sham."

Speech, Rochester, New York, July 4, 1852

This lithograph, "Heroes of the Colored Race," features Frederick Douglass at center. Beside him are Blanche Kelso Bruce (left) and Hiram R. Revels (right), who were elected to Congress after the Civil War.

him back to Baltimore. Two years later, Frederick turned his dream into reality. Disguised as a sailor, he escaped to New York City. Soon afterward he married Anna Murray, a free black woman, and they moved to the seaport of New Bedford, Massachusetts.

Living now as a free man, Frederick took on a new last name, Douglass. He found work as a laborer in New Bedford's shipyards, and in his spare time he continued to read and educate himself. He began attending antislavery meetings in black churches, and he started speaking out about the evils of slavery. In 1841, 23-year-old Frederick Douglass gave a speech at the Massachusetts Anti-Slavery Society's annual convention in Nantucket. His words about his life as a slave moved his audience to tears. Society officials were so impressed by Douglass's eloquence that they hired him as a lecturer.

Over the next four years, Douglass delivered hundreds of speeches throughout the North. So extraordinary were his speaking skills that he became one of the most famous men in America. His words convinced more and more Northerners of the need to put an end to slavery. Not everyone welcomed his message, however. Sometimes Douglass and his abolitionist colleagues were greeted with taunts, rotten eggs, and violence. Moreover, every time Douglass appeared in public he risked being seized as a runaway slave.

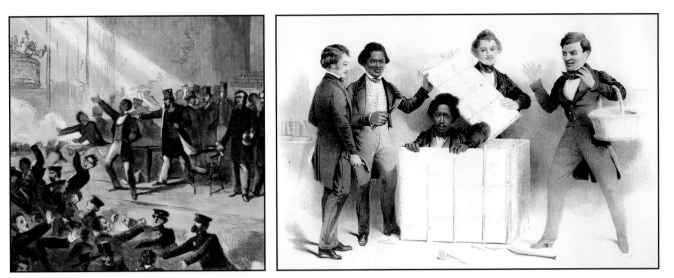

Not all Northerners liked Douglass's antislavery message. When he spoke in Boston in 1860, a proslavery mob interrupted the meeting (above left). As an agent of the Underground Railroad, Douglass helped escaping slaves. The drawing above right shows Douglass (second from left) greeting Henry "Box" Brown, a runaway who had himself shipped in a crate from Richmond to Philadelphia.

Douglass was so well spoken and intelligent that some people began to doubt he had ever been a slave. In response, he wrote his autobiography, *Narrative of the Life of Frederick Douglass*. Published in 1845, the book soon became a best seller, which increased the chances that Douglass would be captured and returned to his former master. To avoid this, he left America for a lecture tour of Great Britain. While he was there, his British friends raised the money to purchase his freedom.

In 1847 Frederick Douglass returned to America. He moved his family to Rochester, New York, and founded the *North Star*, which not only promoted abolitionism but women's rights as well. He continued to agitate, or stir up, the nation's conscience. In a speech given on the Fourth of July in 1852, he pointed out the hypocrisy of the American government. "The existence of slavery in this country," he

Frederick Douglass with his grandson, Joseph.

declared, "brands your republicanism as a sham, your humanity as a base pretense, and your Christianity as a lie."

During the Civil War, Douglass met with President Lincoln to urge him to make emancipation a goal of the war. He also recruited black soldiers for the Union Army. When these troops faced discrimination, he protested to Lincoln on their behalf. After the war, Douglass served a number of government appointments and was later made a minister to Haiti. He also pressed tirelessly for equal citizenship rights—including voting rights—for African Americans.

Honored today for his eloquence, bravery, and the crucial role he played in helping to end slavery, Frederick Douglass fought for reform causes until the end of his life. Shortly before his death in 1895, he gave this advice to a young black man who asked what could be done about racism: "Agitate! Agitate! Agitate!"

Elizabeth Cady Stanton and Susan B. Anthony

THE FRIENDSHIP BETWEEN Elizabeth Cady Stanton and Susan B. Anthony lasted more than 50 years. So did their commitment to women's rights. Together they led the fight for a right that most American women today take for granted: the right to vote.

Stanton was born into a wealthy family in upstate New York in 1815. Her father, Daniel Cady, was a prominent judge. When she was 11, her only brother died, leaving her father crushed by grief. To make up for the loss of her brother, Elizabeth decided to do everything he had done. She jumped over fences on horseback and excelled at school, taking top honors in Greek—highly unusual accomplishments for a girl back then. Although he was proud of his daughter, Judge Cady refused to let her go to college. After all, college was for men. Not only that, he worried that too much education might scare away prospective husbands. Well-bred young women like Elizabeth were expected above all to marry.

In 1840 Elizabeth did indeed marry, but on her own terms. She insisted that the part about the wife obeying the husband be dropped from the wedding vows. Her groom, Henry Brewster Stanton, a lawyer and abolitionist, agreed. Elizabeth shared his abhorrence of slavery and planned to work with him to help abolish it.

Soon after their marriage, the couple traveled to London, where Henry was a delegate to the World Anti-Slavery Convention. There Elizabeth met the famous American abolitionist Lucretia Mott. When the male delegates refused to let women participate at the meeting, Elizabeth and Lucretia faced facts: Slaves weren't the only ones

Friends for more than 50 years, Elizabeth Cady Stanton (seated) and Susan B. Anthony led the fight for a woman's right to vote. They kept up the struggle until the end, as illustrated in the cartoon above, which shows an elderly Anthony chasing President Grover Cleveland for her right to vote. Uncle Sam, symbol of the U.S. government, laughs in the background.

Stanton, Anthony, and other suffragists often faced ridicule from the male-dominated press of their time. This political cartoon from 1896, called "The Apotheosis of Suffrage," made fun of them by suggesting that they deserved the same glory as George Washington. (Apotheosis means raising someone to the rank of a god.) Today the two women truly are honored for their contributions to the nation.

denied justice. The new friends resolved to launch a women's rights movement in the United States.

Elizabeth Cady Stanton had long known that women in America had little or no say in their own lives. According to the law, a married woman could not own property. Anything she inherited—a farm, a house, money—became the property of her husband. If she earned any wages, he got those, too. It was very difficult for a woman to get a divorce, even if her husband abused her. And if a couple had children, by law they belonged only to the husband.

Women in those days could not sign a contract or serve on a jury. In some places they couldn't even testify in court. Colleges were closed to women. Most important, women lacked the right to vote, and without the vote, they could not change the laws that oppressed them.

When Stanton and Mott returned to America, their plan for a women's movement moved to the back burner for a while as Stanton gave birth to three sons in short order. But the issue of women's rights was never far from her mind.

In July 1848 Stanton, who was living in Seneca Falls, New York, got together with Mott and three other women. Over tea, the companions talked about how women everywhere suffered because of a lack of equal rights. Stanton decided it was high time to act. She later recalled, "I stirred myself, as well as the rest of the party, to do and dare anything."

Then and there the women began organizing the first women's rights convention. It opened six days later, on July 19, 1848, "to discuss the social, civil and religious condition and rights of Woman." More than 200 women and 40 men attended the Seneca Falls meeting, at which Stanton presented the Declaration of Sentiments she had drafted. Modeled on the Declaration of Independence, the document proclaimed, "We hold these truths to be self-evident: that all men and women are created equal." It went on to charge: "The history of mankind is a history of repeated injuries and usurpations on the part of man toward woman, having in direct object the establishment of an absolute tyranny over her." Finally, Stanton demanded social and political equality for all women—in particular the right to vote. So began the campaign for women's voting rights, or suffrage.

Called the "The Awakening," this 1915 map symbolizes the enlightenment of the western states, which by this time had granted women voting rights. In the eastern half of the nation, women still lacked the ballot. They are portrayed as calling out from the darkness.

The press of the day ridiculed the Declaration of Sentiments, and many clergymen and politicians denounced it. Nonetheless, women across the country began holding their own meetings to air their complaints and call for action. The women's rights revolution really took off, however, when Stanton joined forces with Susan B. Anthony.

Born in 1820 in Adams, Massachusetts, Susan Brownell Anthony came from a family of reformers. Her parents, Daniel and Lucy Read Anthony, were Quakers who supported abolition and women's rights. They provided excellent educations for their daughters as well as their sons. Daniel Anthony encouraged his daughters to be self-reliant, to think and speak for themselves, and to stand up for what they believed in.

Susan certainly did. When she graduated from school, she took a teaching job with the New York State school system. When Anthony learned that she was earning only one-fifth of what male teachers were paid, she protested—and eventually lost her job because of it.

After ten years of teaching, Anthony turned to reform work. She threw herself into the temperance movement, which sought to ban the drinking of alcohol. Temperance supporters believed that drunkenness contributed to many of society's problems, including poverty and the abuse of women and children.

In 1851 Anthony's temperance work took her to Seneca Falls, where she met Stanton. The two women liked each other at once, and they soon became allies in the fight for women's rights. In 1854 they embarked on a campaign to persuade New York State lawmakers to give married women the right to own property, manage their own earnings, and have custody of their children.

Stanton and Anthony made a great team. Stanton, who was tied to home life by motherhood, researched legal matters, drafted pamphlets, plotted strategy, and wrote speeches. Anthony, who never married, crisscrossed the state delivering Stanton's fiery speeches, holding meetings, and going door to door to circulate petitions. As Stanton remarked, "I forged the thunderbolts, and

Carrying on the battle started by Elizabeth Cady Stanton and Susan B. Anthony, protesters in New York City in 1911 march to demand women's rights (above). Stanton's youngest daughter, Harriot Stanton Blatch, shown below as a baby with her famous mother, took up the fight, as did her own daughter.

she [Anthony] fired them." Their efforts paid off: In 1860 the New York State legislature passed a law granting married women rights to property, income, and child custody.

Voting rights, were much harder to obtain. The struggle to win the ballot was put on hold during the Civil War. Stanton and Anthony focused instead on human rights—the abolition of slavery. When the war ended, they lobbied for an amendment to the Constitution that would give voting rights to African Americans and to women. But politicians and many abolitionists told women that votes for freed slaves had priority over votes for women. Stanton and Anthony fumed when the 14th Amendment, promising voting rights to all "male citizens," was ratified.

In 1869 Stanton and Anthony organized the National Woman Suffrage Association (NWSA),

"We demand in the Reconstruction suffrage
for all the citizens of the Republic.
I would not talk of Negroes or women,
but of citizens."

Elizabeth Cady Stanton, letter of January 13, 1868

Often called the Anthony Amendment in honor of Susan B. Anthony (below), the 19th Amendment had to be ratified by three-fourths of the states before it became law. Kentucky's governor signed the amendment in January 1920 (above left). By the presidential election of 1920, the rest of the required 36 states had approved the amendment, enabling women across America to cast their ballot (above right).

with the goal of obtaining a constitutional amendment giving women the vote. The NWSA's tactics were not always admirable. Members, most of whom were white, sharing the prejudices of their time, insisted that educated white women deserved the vote ahead of recent immigrants and African Americans. Moreover, they tried (unsuccessfully) to defeat the passage of the 15th Amendment, which promised citizens the right to vote regardless of "race, color, or previous condition of servitude."

Stanton and Anthony continued their crusade for woman suffrage for the rest of their lives. Seemingly tireless, Anthony traveled throughout the country seeking support for the cause. In 1878 Elizabeth Cady Stanton wrote a woman's suffrage amendment and had it submitted to the U.S. Senate. Sadly, she did not live to see a suffrage amendment passed. She died in 1902.

Susan B. Anthony, who lived four years longer than her dear friend, knew that she would not see voting rights in her lifetime either. But she had "not a shadow of doubt" that the next generation of women's rights leaders would "carry our cause to victory." In one of her last speeches, she declared that "Failure is impossible." In 1920 Congress finally passed the 19th Amendment giving all women in America the right to vote.

"Marriage, to women as to men,
must be a luxury, not a necessity;
an incident of life, not all of it.
And the only possible way to accomplish this
great change is to accord to women equal
power in the making, shaping
and controlling of the circumstances of life."

Susan. B. Anthony, speech, March 1875

INDUSTRY AND EMPIRE

★ 1876–1900 ★

In 1876 America celebrated the hundredth anniversary of the Declaration of Independence. The nation had come a long way in those hundred years and was about to embark on an era of explosive growth. Americans took special pride in new inventions such as the telephone and light bulb.

American manufacturing took off dramatically during this period, thanks to the emergence of industries such as oil refining, steel manufacturing,

1876

The Lakota and their Cheyenne allies dealt a stunning defeat to the U.S. Army at the Battle of Little Bighorn in 1876. Over the next 15 years or so the United States crushed most Indian resistance.

1879

Thomas Alva Edison invented the first practical incandescent light bulb in 1879, then formed a company to bring electric power and light into homes and businesses.

1890

These Lakota survived the massacre at Wounded Knee, on South Dakota's Pine Ridge Reservation in 1890. U.S. troops killed some 200 Lakota women, children, and men who were trying to surrender.

1898

The sinking of the battleship U.S.S. Maine *in Cuba's Havana Harbor in 1898 outraged the nation. Americans believed Spain was responsible for the blast and went to war.*

and electrical power, and to the huge influx of foreign workers. Ten million immigrants arrived in America in between 1876 and 1900. By 1890, the United States had become the world's leading manufacturer. Much of the wealth from these industries went to a new class of powerful and rich businessmen, called "captains of industry" by their admirers and "robber barons" by their critics.

At the same time it was turning into an industrial giant, the U.S. continued to settle the West. This brought new opportunities for many Americans, but it devastated the Indian tribes. In the 1890s the U.S. began to obtain an overseas empire. Pressured by American pineapple and sugar corporations, the

---
★

"We preferred our own way of living.
We were no expense to the government.
All we wanted was peace and to be left alone."

CRAZY HORSE, OGLALA WARRIOR, 1877

★
---

government annexed the islands of Hawaii in 1898—without consulting its native people. In the Spanish-American War, the U.S. gained control of Cuba, Puerto Rico, and the Philippines. Most Americans were pleased with their nation's prominent role in world affairs. But some, known as anti-imperialists, believed the U.S. had no business ruling over other countries or peoples.

By the turn of the century, the United States had become one of the world's most powerful countries. While many people prospered during this era, life was hard for many others. Industrial laborers worked long hours, often under dangerous conditions, for low wages. And African Americans, especially in the South, faced massive educational, economic, and cultural discrimination.

Sitting Bull

BORN circa 1831, near Grand River, Dakota Territory (now in South Dakota)

DIED December 15, 1890, on the Grand River in South Dakota

AGE AT DEATH 59?

OTHER NAMES Tatanka Iyotanka, which means "sitting bull." When he was born, he was named Jumping Badger, but was renamed Slow to match his serious nature.

FAMILY Parents: elder Sitting Bull and Her-Holy-Door

LANDMARKS Sitting Bull's grave was moved in 1953 from North Dakota to near the north-central border of South Dakota.

MILESTONES June 25, 1876: Battle of Little Bighorn.

Did You Know?

- Sitting Bull killed his first buffalo at age ten.
- When he was 14 he fought in his first battle, proving his courage by charging ahead to land the first strike against the enemy tribe.
- As a young man, Sitting Bull earned many more honors in battle, and he became a high-ranking member of the Strong Heart warrior society. He also mastered the ways of a holy man. Sometimes called medicine men, holy men were believed to have a special link with the spirit world.
- In 1883, Sitting Bull was sent to the Standing Rock Reservation, where he hoed the land.
- In Chicago at the 1893 Columbian Exposition, the cabin where Sitting Bull died was on view in an exhibit marking the 400th anniversary of Christopher Columbus's arrival to the New World.
- There is a college named for Sitting Bull located in Fort Yates, North Dakota.

TRUE TO HIS NAME, THE GREAT LAKOTA chief Sitting Bull refused to budge when the United States ordered his people off South Dakota's Great Plains and onto reservations. Instead, he led the Lakota and their Cheyenne allies in the struggle against the white invaders. Along the way he gained two reputations. Many whites of the time saw him as a bloodthirsty savage standing in the way of civilization. To native Americans, however, he was a heroic freedom fighter striving to save his people's land and way of life.

Born around 1831 in present-day South Dakota, Sitting Bull belonged to the Hunkpapa tribe, one of seven branches of the Lakota. He grew up as Plains Indian boys had for centuries: learning to stalk buffalo and fight as a warrior.

Sitting Bull became a war chief of the Hunkpapa around 1857. Like countless chiefs before him, he led raids against other Indian tribes and defended his own tribe's hunting grounds against such traditional rivals as the Crow, the Arikara, and the Shoshone. In the early 1860s, however, Sitting Bull and his warriors began to clash with a new enemy: the U.S. Army.

Some of the Plains tribes signed treaties with the U.S. government and agreed to live on reservations. Other tribes, including

The great Lakota chief Sitting Bull and his warriors wiped out George Custer and his troops at the Battle of Little Bighorn. The bloody defeat shocked white Americans, but for American Indians it was a blow for freedom. In this sketch by an Indian artist, Sitting Bull and Crazy Horse (painted for battle) rally their warriors.

In May 1877 Sitting Bull led his followers into Canada, out of reach of the U.S. Army. That October U.S. general Alfred Terry met with Sitting Bull in a council at Fort Walsh (above). He offered the chief a pardon if he would settle on a reservation in American territory. Sitting Bull angrily refused. The magazine cover at left satirized the U.S. government's approach to Sitting Bull.

Sitting Bull's Hunkpapa, other Lakota, and the Cheyenne, refused to cooperate with the whites. They continued to fight whenever their territory was threatened. Around 1868 these so-called nontreaty bands recognized Sitting Bull—respected for his spiritual power, wisdom, and bravery—as their leader. It was the first time that the fiercely independent tribes had ever singled out one leader above all others.

The conflict between the U.S. Army and the nontreaty tribes (also known as "hostiles") simmered for several years. Then in 1874 gold was discovered in South Dakota's Black Hills. Considered sacred by many tribes, the area had been set aside for the Lakota by a treaty with the United States in 1868. That didn't stop white miners from rushing into the area. Soon the U.S. government, ignoring its own treaty, told the Indians to clear out of the region and report to reservations. When Sitting Bull and his followers refused, the U.S. Army set out to drive them off the Plains.

In response, the nontreaty tribes gathered together at Sitting Bull's camp in Montana territory and prepared to strike back. On June 25, 1876, Lieutenant Colonel George Armstrong Custer and 265 troops attacked Sitting Bull's camp near the Little Bighorn River. Some 2,000 well-armed warriors were waiting for them. Led by

Sitting Bull was very proud of his large family, five members of which are pictured above in front of a tipi. He had two wives and at least eight children. In an odd twist of history, Sitting Bull toured with William F. "Buffalo Bill" Cody's Wild West Show for four months in 1885 (above right). White audiences cheered wildly the man they had once condemned as a bloodthirsty savage.

Sitting Bull and Oglala chief Crazy Horse, they surrounded Custer and his men and killed them all.

The bloody defeat at Little Bighorn shocked the American public. The government sent many more troops to pursue the defiant tribes, which split up after the battle. Chief after chief surrendered. Sitting Bull and his followers crossed the border into Canada in 1877, where they hunted buffalo on the plains. But the buffalo began to die out, and his people began to starve. Sitting Bull finally gave up. He surrendered to the U.S. Army in July 1881. After being jailed for two years as a prisoner of war, he rejoined his remaining band at the Standing Rock Reservation in South Dakota.

In 1890 Sitting Bull was accused of stirring unrest. As Indian policemen went to arrest the old chief, shooting broke out. When the smoke cleared, Sitting Bull, seven of his followers, and six policemen lay dead. To this day, Sitting Bull's devotion to his people is remembered and honored.

"What treaty that the white man ever made with us have they kept? Not one."

Date unknown

Chief Joseph

BORN	circa 1840, Wallowa Valley, Oregon Territory
DIED	Sept. 21, 1904, Colville Reservation, Washington
AGE AT DEATH	64?
OTHER NAMES	In-mu-too-yah-lat-lat, which in English means "thunder traveling over the mountains."
FAMILY	He was married four times and had nine children, including a set of twins.
LANDMARKS	Nez Perce National Historical Park has 38 sites in four states, including Old Chief Joseph Gravesite near Joseph, Oregon.
MILESTONES	October 5, 1877: Surrendered to Col. Nelson Miles

Did You Know?

- The first contact Nez Perce Indians had with whites was with the Lewis and Clark expedition in 1805.
- Chief Joseph was educated in a mission school.
- An autobiographical article by Chief Joseph was published in the journal *North American Review* in 1879. In the article, he wrote, "I believe much trouble and blood would be saved if we opened our hearts more." He also wrote, "It does not require many words to speak the truth."
- After Chief Joseph died, the reservation physician noted his cause of death was a broken heart.
- The Nez Perce bred the famous Appaloosa pony, known for its courage.
- The Chief Joseph Scenic Highway runs along the northeastern edge of Yellowstone National Park.

"TREAT ALL MEN ALIKE. Give them all the same law. Give them all an even chance to live and grow. The earth is the mother of all people, and all people should have equal rights upon it."

The Nez Perce tribe leader known as Chief Joseph delivered these words to politicians in Washington, D.C., in 1879. They echo the ideals of America's Founding Fathers. Yet these rights had been denied the Nez Perce and other Native Americans as the United States expanded westward, breaking treaties and forcing Indians onto ever smaller reservations.

In 1877 the United States ordered all the Nez Perce to leave their rich valley in the Pacific Northwest and move to a reservation in Idaho. Chief Joseph reluctantly agreed. Trouble began when some young Nez Perce warriors killed a group of white settlers. To avoid retaliation, Chief Joseph decided to lead his group of about 700 followers to Canada—and to freedom.

Over the next four months, the Nez Perce fled more than 1,000 miles in a running battle against the U.S. Army. When they were only some 40 miles from the Canadian border, the Indians were finally overcome. Chief Joseph's surrender speech ended with these famous words: "Hear me, my chiefs, I am tired; my heart is sick and sad. From where the sun now stands, I will fight no more forever."

Chief Joseph and his surviving band were sent to Indian Territory in Oklahoma, where many of them sickened and died. He traveled to Washington, D.C., to plead for the return of his people to their valley. Instead, in 1885 the government exiled them to a reservation in Washington State, far from their ancestral home. He died there brokenhearted in 1904. Remembered for his bravery, dignity, and eloquence, Chief Joseph remains a symbol of the tragic fate of America's native people.

After being forced onto a reservation, Chief Joseph dedicated the rest of his life to getting better treatment for his people. In 1879 he appealed to politicians in Washington, D.C.: "We ask to be recognized as men. We ask that the same law shall work alike on all men....Let me be a free man...and I will obey every law."

Andrew Carnegie

Did You Know?

- Andrew didn't attend school until he said he was ready to go, which was when he was nearly eight years old. He had only four years of formal education.
- After immigrating to Pittsburgh, Carnegie's mother tried to make ends meet by mending shoes.
- Carnegie steel was used in the Brooklyn Bridge, the Washington Monument, and in the New York City elevated railroad, and in skyscrapers and other buildings across the nation.
- One of Carnegie's most famous expressions is, "Put all your eggs in one basket and then watch that basket."
- Carnegie lived with his mother until she died, then married at age 51.
- Carnegie's 1886 book, *Triumphant Democracy*, argued that democracy was the best political system for making money.

ANDREW CARNEGIE ROSE FROM POVERTY to become the richest man in the world. Today he is mostly remembered for his generous philanthropy. In his own time, however, many people despised him for his ruthless approach to business.

Born in the small Scottish village of Dunfermline, Andrew Carnegie was the son of William Carnegie, a handloom weaver, and his wife, Margaret. The family fell on hard times in the 1840s, when economic depression clutched Britain and new steam-powered looms took business away from skilled craftsman like William. The Carnegies decided to seek a better life for themselves in America. After selling off their belongings, they borrowed the rest of the money needed for the journey and set sail for America in May 1848. Andy was 12 years old.

The family settled in Pittsburgh. William took a job in a textile mill. Andy did, too. "I fairly panted to get to work that I might help the family to a start in the new land," he recalled. At night he studied bookkeeping, and he read to educate himself. He believed that in America there was no end to what a smart, hardworking, and ambitious young man like himself could achieve.

When he was 14 Andy got a job as a messenger with a telegraph office. He taught himself Morse code, was promoted to telegraph operator, and soon became the fastest operator in the office, as well as the main breadwinner for his family. At age 17 Andy caught the notice of a superintendent of the Pennsylvania Railroad, who hired him

Self-made millionaire Andrew Carnegie liked to say, "The man who dies rich, dies disgraced." After retiring from business in 1901, he gave away more than $350 million to worthy causes. He is most famous for funding thousands of free public libraries, shown in the cartoon above as the building blocks of his legacy.

The Washington Public Library, shown here in an architectural drawing, was one of thousands of free public libraries funded by Andrew Carnegie. President Theodore Roosevelt, a friend of Carnegie's, attended the dedication of the library in 1903. Carnegie paid only for the cost of the library buildings. Communities that wanted them had to promise to buy the books for it and operate it at their own expense. This reflected his philosophy that people should help themselves.

as his personal secretary. Bright young Andrew Carnegie showed a flair for business, and quickly advanced his position at the railroad. Meanwhile, he began buying stocks and investing in various business ventures. By age 23, Carnegie had become a railroad superintendent himself.

In 1865 Carnegie left the Pennsylvania Railroad to pursue his own business ventures full-time. "I was determined to make a fortune," he later wrote, "and I saw no means of doing this honestly at any salary the railroad could afford to give." He had already set up an iron manufacturing business and organized a company to build iron bridges, which he foresaw would soon be needed to replace old railroad bridges made of wood.

By 1868, when he was 33 years old, Carnegie's

In 1910 Carnegie, pictured above with British peace advocate Lord Weardale, founded the Carnegie Endowment for International Peace to promote harmony and understanding among nations. Carnegie may have hoped that donating his wealth to such worthy causes would help improve his image. People had not forgotten the deadly violence he authorized at his Homestead steelworks, an event symbolized in this drawing by Thomas Nast, one of the most influential political cartoonists of the age.

> "Upon the sacredness of property civilization itself depends—the right of the laborer to his hundred dollars in the savings bank, and equally the legal right of the millionaire to his millions."
>
> "Wealth," article by Carnegie in *North American Review,* June 1889

annual income was more than $50,000, and he had assets of $400,000. He was proud of his success, yet uncomfortable with his wealth. He wrote a note to himself promising to retire from business in two years and "[take] a part in public matters, especially those connected with education and improvement of the poorer classes."

Greed and hunger for power proved stronger than Carnegie's noble intentions, however. He stayed in business for another three decades, increasing his wealth with each new venture. In the 1860s he moved into the steel industry. Using the latest technologies to turn iron into steel, his mills became the most efficient in the country. He drove his competitors out of business by slashing his own production costs and selling steel for lower prices than anyone else.

Carnegie liked to think of himself as a friend of the working man, but in reality he underpaid his steel-mill workers, most of whom were immigrants from southern Europe. In 1892 thousands of workers at his huge steelworks in Homestead, Pennsylvania, went on strike. At the time Carnegie was in Scotland, but he authorized his top aide, Henry Clay Frick, to use whatever means necessary to

At age 51, Carnegie married Louise Whitfield. They divided their time between his castle in Scotland and their home in New York City.

smash the union. Frick brought in private guards known as Pinkertons, and a bloody battle erupted. Several men on both sides were killed and many more were wounded. In the end, the plant reopened with cheaper, nonunion labor, but the incident tarnished Carnegie's reputation.

In 1901 Andrew Carnegie finally kept his promise to himself to retire and turn his attention to public affairs. He sold his steel empire to financier J.P. Morgan for $480 million (about $12.5 billion today) and devoted his energies to philanthropy. Carnegie believed that the wealthy had an obligation to give back to society. Perhaps he also hoped that his generosity would help him shed his image as a "robber baron."

He funded educational institutions in Scotland and the United States, cultural institutions such as theaters and music halls, and scientific research. He founded nearly 3,000 free public libraries, most of them in the United States. He gave $50,000 to scientist Marie Curie for her research on radium. A committed pacifist, Carnegie established foundations to promote world peace. By the time he died in 1919 at the age of 83, he'd given away nearly $350 million and become one of the greatest philanthropists of all time.

Queen Lili'uokalani

★

BORN	September 2, 1838, Honolulu, Hawaii
DIED	November 11, 1917, Honolulu, Hawaii
AGE AT DEATH	79
OTHER NAMES	Lydia Kamakaeha, Lydia Lili'uokalani (lih-lee-ah-WOE-keh-LAHN-ee) Paki
FAMILY	Married John Owen Dominis in 1862. They had no children.
LANDMARKS	Lili'uokalani Garden in Honolulu, Hawaii
MILESTONES	July 1898: The United States annexed the Hawaiian Islands.

Did You Know?

- Lili'uokalani was a talented musician and composer. She composed 165 pieces, and wrote one of Hawaii's most famous songs, "Aloha 'Oe." Lili'uokalani later wrote in her memoirs that "to compose was as natural to me as to breathe. This gift remains a source of the greatest consolation."
- Lili'uokalani attended Queen Victoria's Golden Jubilee in London in 1887 and was welcomed as royalty by the queen herself. On the way to London, Lili'uokalani visited Washington, D.C., where she was received by President Grover Cleveland.
- She helped lead the movement against annexation. The movement's motto was "Hawaii for the Hawaiians."
- In 1878 she visited California and was impressed by Mills Seminary College. She dreamed of starting a college for women in Hawaii.
- Queen Lili'uokalani translated the Hawaiian creation myth (about how the world was created) into English.
- The Queen Lili'uokalani Trust assists poor and orphaned children.

WHEN QUEEN LILI'UOKALANI assumed the Hawaiian throne in 1891, the island kingdom was on the brink of being taken over by the United States. She did her best to prevent it.

Born into a royal family, Lili'u attended a special school for royal children, run by American missionaries. She became fluent in English and also learned American manners. But she never forgot her native tongue or lost her pride in Hawaiian traditions. When she was 24, she married an American named John Owen Dominis.

Despite her husband's nationality, Lili'u criticized the increasing power Americans had in Hawaii. They owned almost all the sugar plantations and were trying to control the kingdom's affairs.

In 1874 Lili'uokalani's brother, David Kalakaua, became king. In 1887 white business leaders forced him to sign a new constitution at gunpoint. It severely limited the monarch's authority, put great power in the hands of the American members of his cabinet, and deprived most Hawaiians of the right to vote.

When King Kalakaua died in 1891, Lili'uokalani was declared Hawaii's first queen. One of her first acts was to try to do away with the so-called bayonet constitution. She had a new constitution drafted that returned power to native Hawaiians. Meanwhile, the wealthy American community plotted to overthrow her. In 1893 they called in U.S. Marines, who marched down the streets of Honolulu and stationed themselves in front of the royal palace. Queen Lili'uokalani was forced to surrender, and the Americans proclaimed a new government.

Hawaii was annexed as an American territory in 1898. Lili'uokalani, like most Hawaiians, refused to watch the ceremony in which the Hawaiian flag was lowered and the Stars and Stripes raised in its place. She died 19 years after the takeover. Hawaii's last monarch, Queen Lili'uokalani is honored now as she was in her lifetime for her efforts to preserve Hawaiian independence.

Lili'uokalani was Hawaii's first queen and last monarch. She came from a long line of royal chiefs, who were honored by the Hawaiians as gods. Today Queen Lili'uokalani is praised for her efforts to prevent the overthrow of the Hawaiian kingdom by the United States and to preserve Hawaiian traditions, including ancient chants.

Alexander Graham Bell

BORN March 3, 1847, Edinburgh, Scotland

DIED August 2, 1922, Beinn Bhreagh, Cape Breton Island, Nova Scotia, Canada

AGE AT DEATH 75

FAMILY Parents: Alexander Melville Bell and Eliza Bell. Wife: Mabel Hubbard; two daughters: Elsie May and Marian. Elsie May married Gilbert Grosvenor, who became the first president of the National Geographic Society.

LANDMARKS Alexander Graham Bell National Historic Site, Nova Scotia, Canada

HONORS 1880: Volta Prize from France

Did You Know?

- The "Graham" in Bell's name wasn't added until he was 11 years old.
- The race to patent the telephone was intense; Bell submitted his plans a mere two hours before his chief rival.
- Bell showed his new invention, the telephone, at the Centennial Exhibition in Philadelphia, Pennsylvania, on June 25, 1876—the same day as the Battle of Little Bighorn, where Sitting Bull (*see pages 84–87*) and his fighters defeated Lt. Col. George Custer.
- Bell's hydrofoil set a speed record that lasted for ten years. In 1919 it traveled almost 71 miles per hour.
- Bell held 18 patents on his own and 12 more with collaborators.
- It wasn't until January 1915 that a telephone call could be made from New York to California. This coast-to-coast call took place with the help of 130,000 telephone poles.

INVENTING THE TELEPHONE made Alexander Graham Bell famous. But it was his boundless energy, passion for science and inventing, and commitment to improving the quality of life for people everywhere that made him truly extraordinary.

Born and raised in Edinburgh, Scotland, Alexander—called Alec—came from a family of communicators. His grandfather Bell was a well-known speech teacher in London. Alec's father, Melville Bell, also taught speech. In addition, he studied how the human voice produces sound. Melville's research led him to create a universal phonetic alphabet—a system of symbols that represented any sound the human voice could make. He called this system "visible speech."

Alec's mother kindled her son's interest in music. She was a talented pianist, despite being very nearly deaf. By putting one end of her ear tube on the piano's soundboard, she could hear, or feel, the vibrations of the music. Alec grew up fascinated by sounds and how they are made. He also loved exploring nature.

At age 11, Alec made his first invention. He was playing at a gristmill when the miller challenged him to do something useful. After experimenting for a while, Alec devised a hand-cranked tool that took the tough husks off wheat kernels.

When Alec was 16, he visited London with his father. There they saw a "speaking machine"—a device that mechanically produced vocal sounds. Alec was so intrigued by it that Melville Bell challenged him and his older brother, Melly, to make one of their own. After studying the larynx, or voice box, of a dead sheep, the

Best known for inventing the telephone, Alexander Graham Bell was fascinated by "the world and all that is in it." A founding father of the National Geographic Society, he remarked, "The study of Nature is undoubtedly one of the most interesting of all pursuits. God has strewn our paths with wonders, and we certainly should not go through Life with our eyes shut."

brothers built a model of the vocal organs. To their delight, it actually worked.

While still a teenager, Alec landed a job teaching music and elocution, or public speaking, at a boy's boarding school in northern Scotland. During this time he investigated the pitch, or vibrating speed, of vowel sounds using musical tuning forks. He found that each vowel had a unique rate of vibration. Then he discovered that the famous German scientist Hermann von Helmholtz had already made the same discovery. From reviewing von Helmholtz's research, Alec got the idea that sounds could be transmitted through a wire. Actually, he misunderstood Helmholtz's diagrams, but it was a lucky mistake. Bell later described this as a "very valuable blunder," which set him on the path that led to the invention of the telephone.

Tragedy struck the Bell family in 1867, when Alec's younger brother, Edward, died from tuberculosis. Three years later Melly died from the same disease. Seeking a healthier climate, Alec and his parents moved to Ontario, Canada.

In 1871, Alec began teaching at a school for deaf children in Boston, Massachusetts. Using his father's visible speech system, he helped the students learn to speak. Bell found great joy in working with the deaf.

Built by Thomas Watson from a sketch drawn by Bell in 1875, this gallows telephone—named for its shape—was the first device to transmit complex sounds.

In 1892, a group of businessmen watched Bell make the first call from New York to Chicago. By 1917 the Bell long-distance network wired most of the nation.

He believed it was his true calling. Even after he invented the telephone, he listed "teacher of the deaf" as his profession, and he did so the rest of his life. One of his pupils in Boston, Mabel Hubbard, eventually became his wife.

Boston was an exciting place for someone interested in communication. The leading center of American electrical technology, it was full of inventors. Many of them were trying to find a way to send more than one message at a time over a single telegraph wire. Bell had his own ideas about how to improve the telegraph. A night owl, he experimented in the evenings, when he had finished teaching. He kept thinking about his idea of sending speech over a wire. He theorized that the rising and falling pitches of the human voice could be converted into a rising and falling, or undulatory, electric current that could be transmitted over a wire. At the end of the wire a receiving device could convert the electrical energy back into sound.

To find out whether his ideas would work, Bell needed supplies and a technician who could build models. In January 1875, Bell hired 20-year-old Thomas Watson, a skilled craftsman and electrician, as his assistant. Watson turned Bell's sketches into machines.

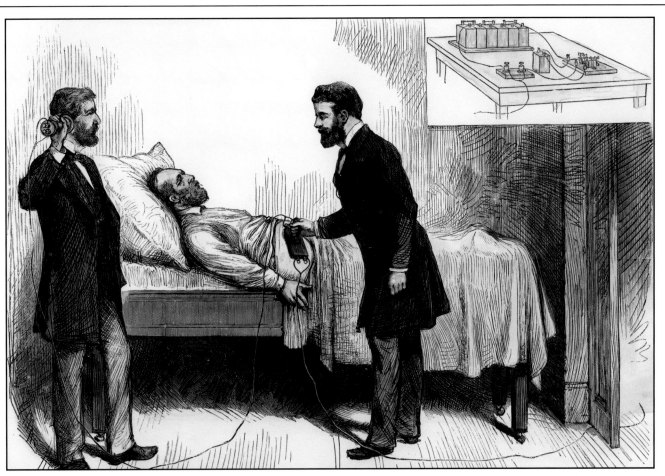

In this drawing Bell and an assistant use a metal-detecting machine invented by Bell to find the assassin's bullet in President Garfield. Although his efforts failed to help Garfield, Bell later developed a telephonic probe that was used in military hospitals to save soldiers' lives. "Certainly no man can have a higher incentive," he said, "than the hope of relieving suffering and saving life."

In their quest to send vocal sound over a wire, Bell and Watson tried dozens of combinations of electric current and materials to transmit it. Progress was slow, but Bell remained confident. "I think the transmission of the human voice is much more nearly at hand than I had supposed," he wrote. The breakthrough came on March 10, 1876. On that day he spoke these now-famous words into his latest design: "Mr. Watson—Come here—I want to see you." To Bell's delight, Watson heard and understood his words through a duplicate device in another room. It was the first telephone call.

Three months later, Bell introduced the telephone to the public at the Centennial Exhibition in Philadelphia. The emperor of Brazil was so impressed by the demonstration that he ordered one hundred telephones for his country.

In 1877, Alexander Graham Bell and Mabel Hubbard were married. They honeymooned in

"I believe that in the future...a man in one part of the Country may communicate by word of mouth with another in a distant place."

Prospectus to British financiers, March 5, 1878

Alexander Graham Bell met his future wife, Mabel Hubbard (above left), when her parents hired him to teach her to speak as normally as possible. She had lost her hearing at age five. Bell met Helen Keller, who was blind and deaf, when she was six years old. The two of them, shown above right with Helen's teacher, Annie Sullivan, became lifelong friends.

England, where Alec took pride in demonstrating his remarkable invention. In the meantime, Mabel's father helped lead the new Bell Telephone Company.

When the Bells returned to the United States the following year, they brought with them a baby daughter. For a while, Bell helped advise the company that bore his name, but he refused to limit himself to that line of work. Fortunately, the money he earned from the company gave him the freedom "to follow the ideas that interest me most."

And that's just what he did for the rest of his life. He pursued his love of science and he kept on inventing. In 1881, Bell worked around the clock to come up with a device that might help save the life of President James Garfield. He was slowly dying from an assassin's bullet that lay too deep for surgeons to find. Bell invented two metal-detecting machines. Although neither invention saved Garfield's life, one of them went on to be used in military

hospitals and saved countless soldiers' lives.

The same year, the Bells' newborn son died from breathing problems. Alec's grief led him to develop another life-saving invention. Called a "vacuum jacket," it used a pump to force air into and out of the lungs. It was a forerunner of the iron lung, which was developed for polio victims five decades later.

In the early 1880s, Bell underwrote a project to develop an improved version of the phonograph, which had been invented by Thomas Edison. The sale of the patents on these inventions brought Bell $200,000. He used the money to fund research on deafness.

Throughout his life, Bell remained devoted to his work for and with the deaf. He became a leader in the education of deaf children and enjoyed visiting them at their schools. He became a great friend of the blind and deaf Helen Keller *(see pages 120–123)*, who dedicated her autobiography to him. Bell studied the scientific causes of deafness and investigated

At Beinn Breagh, his summer estate in Nova Scotia, Canada, Bell pursued his interest in flight by designing and flying huge kites, such as the tetrahedral kite shown above left. He enjoyed having his grandchildren join him at Beinn Breagh. He frolicked with them in the bay (above, Bell on the dock at far right), and led the family in singalongs at the piano in the evenings.

whether heredity might play a role. He also invented the audiometer, which measures a person's hearing.

Bell's summer estate in Nova Scotia, Canada, gave him room to indulge his interest in flight, which had long intrigued him. "The more I experiment," he wrote in 1893, "the more convinced I become that flying machines are practical." He designed and flew huge kites and tested different shapes. He found that the tetrahedron—a pyramid-like group of triangles—produced the lightest and strongest kites. He predicted that the form would find use "for all sorts of constructing—a new method of architecture." He was right. Today, tetrahedral cells are common building blocks in what is known as space-frame architecture.

> "The inventor is a man who looks around upon the world and...wants to improve whatever he sees."
>
> Speech to patent congress in Washington, D.C., 1891

When he was in his 70s, Bell and a young assistant began to experiment with hydrofoils, boats that move just above the water. One of their models set a world water-speed record that stood for ten years. Energetic to the end, Bell was working on a way to extract drinkable water from the air—an invention that he hoped might aid people adrift at sea—shortly before his death.

Alexander Graham Bell once said that a true inventor "can no more help inventing than he can help thinking or breathing." This was certainly true of Bell himself. When he died in 1922, the phone company silenced all telephones for one minute in tribute to the man whose most famous invention, in the words of Thomas Edison, "brought the human family in closer touch."

George Washington Carver

Did You Know?

- Carver reportedly declined a $100,000 salary offer to work for Thomas Edison in his lab.
- Carver originally wanted to become an artist. In later life he taught people how to use native clays to make paints.
- Carver lived very simply at Tuskegee. He founded the George Washington Carver Foundation with the money he saved—almost $60,000. Today Tuskegee University carries on his legacy, where researchers work on the genetic engineering of foods, including the sweet potato.
- Carver is credited with creating about 300 products from peanuts and more than 100 products from sweet potatoes.
- His work helped hundreds of poor black farmers improve their economic situation.

IN THE LATE 1800S, POOR BLACK SHARECROPPERS in the South barely scratched a living out of the soil. Bad harvests year after year left most of them crushed by debt. Scientist George Washington Carver made it his goal to help them.

Carver was born a slave toward the end of the American Civil War. At around age ten he left his former owners, who had raised him, and roamed the Midwest, working odd jobs and seeking an education wherever blacks were allowed to attend school. He eventually enrolled at Iowa State Agricultural College, and in 1896 he graduated with a master's degree in agriculture.

Carver accepted an offer to head the agricultural department at Tuskegee Institute, an African-American college in Alabama. He worked on ways to help farmers get the most out of the land. Decades of growing cotton and tobacco had robbed the soil of nutrients. Carver urged farmers to rotate crops—to alternate cotton and tobacco with peanuts and sweet potatoes, which put nutrients back into the soil. To spread his message, he and his students traveled the countryside demonstrating his farming techniques.

Southern farmers soon produced bumper crops of peanuts. To create a market for them and highlight their versatility, Carver made unusual products with peanuts, such as ink, cheese, and soap. He also developed flour, rubber, and postage stamp glue from sweet potatoes. As word of his accomplishments spread, he became one of the most admired men in America. Carver stayed at Tuskegee until his death in 1943.

A talented teacher and scientist, George Washington Carver (above, in his laboratory), wrote that his ideal was "to be of the greatest good to the greatest number of 'my people' possible." He thought the best way to empower African Americans was through a practical education, which could "unlock the golden door of freedom to our people."

PROGRESSIVISM AND THE NEW DEAL

★ 1900–1941 ★

America entered the 20th century with enormous optimism and pride. Manufacturing, commerce, and trade were booming, and the U.S. was flexing its muscle as a dominant world power. Yet some Americans worried that too many people were shut out of the nation's prosperity. Their concerns brought about an age of reform, in which people throughout the country worked to make America a better place for everyone.

1908

Henry Ford ushered in the automobile age with the mass-produced Model T in 1908. At $850.00, the car was priced so that even people of average income could afford to buy one.

1920

Suffragists rejoiced when the 19th Amendment was finally passed in 1920. Winning the right to vote was part of a 72-year struggle on the part of thousands of women.

1930–1940

During the Great Depression, millions were unemployed and poverty was widespread. This photo of a poor migrant mother and her children has become a symbol of the time.

1938

Children had been used as a source of cheap labor in U.S. factories and mines since the days of the industrial revolution. Congress finally outlawed child labor in 1938.

The years 1900 to 1914 are known as the Progressive Era. Progressives supported a variety of reforms. They worked to outlaw child labor and to improve conditions for millions living in city slums, many of whom were recent immigrants. They campaigned for safety standards in food and for safer conditions in factories. Progressives called for regulations to make big business more competitive and less politically powerful. They crusaded against government corruption. And they were among the first to encourage protection of wilderness areas. Most Progressives also supported voting rights for women, although few showed much interest in equality for African Americans.

★

"Our nation, glorious in youth and strength, looks into the future with eager eyes and rejoices as a strong man to run a race."

THEODORE ROOSEVELT, REPUBLICAN CONVENTION, 1900

★

As many of the Progressives' goals passed into law, government came to play a bigger role than ever before in American life. Not everyone was pleased by this. Conservatives believed government should stay out of the way and let big business generate profits that would trickle down to everyone.

Economic prosperity continued into the 1920s, and incomes for nearly everyone rose. Many Americans bought automobiles. In October 1929 the good times ended abruptly, when the stock market crashed and the country fell into the deepest economic depression in U.S. history. In the New Deal era that followed, government programs to help Americans survive the Depression became more ambitious than any reforms the Progressives had dreamed of.

Wright Brothers

★

WILBUR WRIGHT

BORN April 16, 1867, near Millville, Indiana

DIED May 30, 1912, Dayton, Ohio

AGE AT DEATH 45

ORVILLE WRIGHT

BORN August 19, 1871, Dayton, Ohio

DIED January 30, 1948, Dayton, Ohio

AGE AT DEATH 76

SHARED HISTORY

OTHER NAMES Wilbur was called Ullam and Orville was Bubs.

FAMILY Parents: Milton and Susan Wright.

LANDMARKS Wright Brothers National Memorial, Kill Devil Hills, North Carolina Smithsonian National Air and Space Museum, Washington, D.C., has the original *Flyer*.

MILESTONES October 1905: The first public demonstration of flight happened in Dayton, Ohio.

HONORS 1909: Congressional Medal of Honor and French Legion of Honor

Did You Know?

- Wilbur cared for his dying mother, who had tuberculosis. She died in 1889.
- Wilbur and Orville owned a cat named Old Mom when they were children. When Wilbur adopted a stray dog in 1908, he named it Flyer.
- Wilbur never graduated from high school.
- The first powered flight on December 17, 1903, was 120 feet long, with an airspeed of 34 mph. The brothers made three more powered flights that morning.
- In September 1908, Orville was working with the U.S. Army when a propeller split and the airplane crashed. His passenger, Thomas Selfridge, died—the first casualty of powered flight.

IN DECEMBER 1903 Wilbur and Orville Wright did what no human being had done before: They flew. This stunning feat ushered in the age of powered flight and made the Wright brothers the first American heroes of the 20th century.

Wilbur was born in 1867. Orville came along four years later. Their father, a minister, moved his family all over the Midwest before finally settling in Dayton, Ohio. The frequent moves helped make the Wrights a tight-knit family. Wilbur and Orville were particularly close. As Wilbur recalled, he and Orville "lived together, played together, worked together, and, in fact, thought together....nearly everything that was done in our lives has been the result of conversations, suggestions, and discussions between us."

Both brothers loved to tinker. When he was 17, Orville started a printing business using a press he made out of odds and ends. Wilbur soon joined the venture, and he and Orville built a bigger press. The odd-looking contraption, which included the top of an old buggy carriage, could print one thousand sheets an hour. Soon the Wright brothers were producing everything from business cards to newsletters.

Three years later the brothers branched out and opened a bicycle shop in Dayton. They quickly jumped from selling and repairing bicycles to designing and manufacturing their own models based on the latest technology. The business was a success,

Among the qualities that helped Orville (far left) and Wilbur Wright solve the mystery of flight was bravery. Every time they flew the brothers took enormous risks. The 1903 Flyer, built at the Wrights' bicycle shop in Dayton, Ohio (above), was especially dangerous because its engine and propellers made it heavier than anything they had flown before.

and yet the brothers, especially Wilbur, were restless. They wanted more of a challenge. They found it in the mystery of flight.

Wilbur and Orville first took an interest in flight when they were children and their father brought home a toy helicopter. Powered by rubber bands, the little flying machine lifted itself into the air. The young boys were fascinated. As grown men their interest in flying was rekindled in 1896, the year that German glider pioneer Otto Lilienthal died while testing one of his gliders. Wondering what had caused the fatal crash, they talked about Lilienthal's work. One thing led to another, and the brothers decided to build their own full-size flying machine.

The Wrights read through everything their local library and the Smithsonian had to offer on aeronautics, the science of flight. After studying these materials, Wilbur concluded that in order to build a flying machine that would actually fly, he and Orville would have to solve the problem of control.

In the workroom behind their bicycle shop, the brothers started building giant kites and gliders to test their design ideas. They focused on creating a mechanical system that would allow a pilot to control an aircraft up, down, and around. They experimented with flexible tail rudders, a third small wing, and flexible wings. Along the way they invented the technology they needed to build their flying machines.

The Wrights began flying, and crashing, gliders in 1900 (top). In 1908 and 1909 they made hundreds of exhibition flights in powered planes (middle and bottom).

To test wing curvatures, for example, they built their own wind tunnel using a six-foot-long wooden box, bicycle spokes, old hacksaw blades, and a belt-operated fan.

In 1900 the Wrights traveled to the village of Kitty Hawk, on North Carolina's Outer Banks, to test their first full-scale glider. The location provided steady winds, sand dunes from which to launch their aircraft, a soft landing place, and privacy. Back home in Dayton, they modified their designs based on their test findings.

Wilbur and Orville returned to Kitty Hawk in 1901 and 1902 to conduct tests with new, improved gliders. Lying flat on their bellies atop their machines to cut down on wind resistance, the brothers took turns coasting over the sand again and again. In 1902 they made more than 250 flights. By the time they left Kitty Hawk, they had mastered the problem of control enough to take the next step. They were ready to build and fly a powered airplane.

Once the Wright brothers built a light-weight engine for their first *Flyer,* it was back to Kitty Hawk. On December 17, 1903, with Orville at the controls, *Flyer* lifted off from the ground on its own power and flew 120 feet. The 12-second flight proved that humans could fly.

After their success with *Flyer,* the Wright brothers devoted themselves to building a practical airplane they could sell. By 1905 they had made a plane that stayed in the air for 39 minutes

Launched into the air by his brother and an assistant, Wilbur Wright coasts over sand dunes near Kitty Hawk, North Carolina, in the 1902 glider. He made the world's first controlled turn in a flying machine in this glider. The following year, Orville Wright made the first controlled powered flight ever in the 1903 Flyer.

and survived repeated takeoffs and landings. In 1908 they signed contracts to build airplanes for the U.S. military and French investors, and the world learned of their amazing invention. Within a few years, the brothers were international celebrities. Wilbur had only a few years to enjoy their success. He died of typhoid fever in 1912. Orville lived until 1948.

The secrets of flight had baffled great minds for centuries. Wilbur and Orville Wright focused all their intellectual and engineering skills on finding the answers. When they did, it changed the world.

"While thousands of the most dissimilar body structures, such as insects, fishes, reptiles, birds, and mammals were flying every day at pleasure, it was reasonable to suppose that man also might fly."

Wilbur Wright, 1912

Orville Wright

Wilbur Wright

Theodore Roosevelt

BORN	October 27, 1858, New York, New York
DIED	January 6, 1919, Oyster Bay, New York
AGE AT DEATH	60
OTHER NAMES	Teddy, T.R.
FAMILY	Six children. His first wife, Alice Hathaway Lee, died in 1884. His second wife and First Lady was Edith Kermit Carow. His son Quentin died in combat in World War I.
LANDMARKS	Mount Rushmore, South Dakota. Theodore Roosevelt Island, Washington, D.C. Sagamore Hill National Historic Site, Oyster Bay, New York
HONORS	1905: Nobel Peace Prize for negotiating peace between Russia and Japan

Did You Know?

- Roosevelt dealt with other governments by thinking of the United States as a police force that would act if the nation felt threatened. This was known as "Big Stick Diplomacy."
- Many people criticized his role in expanding America's empire.
- T.R. charged into office with the same enthusiasm that made him a war hero, and he wowed the public with his boundless energy and keen intellect. In the 1904 election, he won by a landslide.
- After leaving office, T.R. went on safari in Africa and collected hundreds of animals for the Smithsonian Institution. He also spent seven months exploring the jungles of Brazil.
- Roosevelt was a respected ornithologist.
- Sagamore Hill, the Roosevelt's home, was known as the "summer White House."

To THEODORE ROOSEVELT, AMERICA'S WILDERNESS areas were a major part of the nation's "rich heritage." He believed such places should be "preserved for [Americans'] children and their children's children forever with their majestic beauty unmarred." He used his power as President to help make that happen.

Teddy Roosevelt was born into a wealthy New York family in 1858. After the death of his first wife in 1884, he moved west and took up cowboy life in the Dakota Territory. Two years later barrel-chested Teddy returned to the East Coast, remarried, and plunged into politics. When the Spanish-American War broke out, he recruited a cavalry company and headed for combat in Cuba. Colonel Roosevelt and his "Rough Riders" became famous for their daring charge near San Juan Hill.

After the war Roosevelt was elected governor of New York, then became William McKinley's Vice President. In September 1901 McKinley was assassinated, and Roosevelt was sworn in as the youngest President ever at age 42.

Progressive-minded T.R. injected government regulation into such areas as industry, labor, and consumer protection. He became known as a "trust-buster" for breaking up monopolies, or trusts, of companies that dominated certain businesses and prevented competition. T.R.'s most far-sighted achievements, however, may have been his preservation of more than 150 million acres of government land—a legacy for which he is admired to this day.

COL. ROOSEVELT Tells the story of THE ROUGH RIDERS in Scribner's Magazine. It begins in January and will run for six months, with many illustrations from photographs taken in the field.
JANUARY SCRIBNER'S
NOW READY PRICE 25 CENTS

President Theodore Roosevelt stands before the wonders of California's Yosemite Valley. Devoted to environmental conservation, Roosevelt created 150 national forests, 53 federal bird sanctuaries, and 5 national parks. As a young cavalry commander, he and his "Rough Riders" gained national attention for his wartime heroism (above).

Jane Addams

★

BORN	September 6, 1860, Cedarville, Illinois
DIED	May 21, 1935, Chicago, Illinois
AGE AT DEATH	74
FAMILY	Father: John Huy Addams, fought in the Civil War and was friends with Abraham Lincoln. Mother: Sarah Weber, died when Jane was two years old.
LANDMARKS	Hull-House, Chicago, Illinois
HONORS	1931: Nobel Peace Prize. Another American, the president of Columbia University, Nicholas Murray Butler, was her co-winner.

Did You Know?

- Under Addams's leadership, Hull-House expanded to include an art gallery, coffeehouse, gymnasium, swimming pool, lending library, and a boardinghouse for working girls.
- Addams threw her support behind Theodore Roosevelt in his bid for President in 1912. Roosevelt ran as a Progressive.
- A devoted pacifist, Jane Addams publicly opposed America's entry into World War I.
- In 1920 Jane Addams helped found the American Civil Liberties Union.
- Addams helped found the Women's Peace Party, which became the Women's International League for Peace and Freedom. The organization has branches in some 50 countries.
- She was the author of several books, including her autobiography, *Twenty Years at Hull-House*.

THE DAUGHTER OF A PROSPEROUS MILL OWNER in Cedarville, Illinois, Jane Addams was no more than six when she first saw the poorest quarter of a neighboring town. It made a lasting impression on her. Before then, she later wrote, it had never occurred to her that all the city's streets were "not as...attractive as the one which contained the glittering toyshop and the confectioner." She could hardly believe that "people lived in such horrid little houses so close together."

When Jane grew up, she devoted her life to helping people rise above such poverty. In 1889 she and a college classmate, Ellen Gates Starr, rented Hull-House, an old mansion in a Chicago working-class district. They moved into it and turned it into a settlement house—a community center for recent immigrants and other residents.

Hull-House provided a variety of services for the poor that could not be found elsewhere at the time, including health care, a kindergarten and nursery for children of working mothers, an employment bureau, and legal services. It offered arts programs, job training, and classes in English and citizenship. It also became a meeting place for clubs and labor unions. Two years after it opened, Hull-House was hosting 2,000 people a week. It became a training ground for new social workers and inspired the creation of more settlement houses throughout the nation.

Over the years, Addams continued to lead Hull-House, and she began to crusade for social reform. She campaigned against child labor and in favor of workers' rights and votes for women. She also became very active in international peace efforts. In 1931 Jane Addams's commitment to improving life for the downtrodden received worldwide recognition, when she became the first American woman to be awarded the Nobel Peace Prize.

Pioneer social worker Jane Addams was among the first generation of women in America to receive a college degree. After college, she attended medical school but dropped out because of health problems. She was inspired to found Hull-House after visiting a settlement house called Toynbee Hall in London.

Matthew Henson

BORN August 8, 1866, Charles County, Maryland

DIED March 9, 1955, New York, New York

AGE AT DEATH 88

FAMILY Henson married twice. He wed his second wife, Lucy Jane Ross, in 1907.

LANDMARKS Matthew Henson Earth Conservation Center, Washington, D.C. Arlington National Cemetery, Arlington, Virginia. Henson and his wife were reinterred here in 1988, alongside Peary.

HONORS 1937: Made a member of the Explorers Club. 1944: Congressional medal. 1996: U.S. Navy named an oceanographic survey ship for Henson. 2000: Hubbard Medal (posthumous)

Did You Know?

- Henson and Peary had 24 men, 130 sled dogs, and 20 sleds with them on their 1909 attempt to reach the North Pole.
- Henson was so fluent in the Inuit language and so adept in their ways that Peary remarked that he was "more of an Eskimo than some of them."
- After his time exploring the northern latitudes, Henson was a customs house clerk in New York City, an appointment made by President William Howard Taft. He worked at the job until 1936.
- Henson's autobiography, *A Negro Explorer at the North Pole,* was published in 1912.
- In the spring of 2005 a team of adventurers retraced Peary's route from base camp to the North Pole to prove that he could have made it in just 37 days—a claim long doubted by critics. The modern team made the 420-mile trip in 36 days, 22 hours, and 11 minutes.

IN THE EARLY 20TH CENTURY, explorers from several nations raced to see who would be first to stand on top of the world at the North Pole. On April 6, 1909, two Americans claimed victory: Commander Robert E. Peary and his right-hand man, African-American explorer Matthew Henson.

Born in Maryland in 1866, Henson signed on as a cabin boy on a sailing ship when he was 12 or 13. After six years at sea, Henson returned to land life. He eventually found work at a hat shop in Washington, D.C. That's where he met Peary. Peary, an engineer and explorer, was preparing for an expedition to Nicaragua, and he hired Henson to go along as his valet. When they returned, Peary asked Henson to join him on a quest for the Pole. Adventure-loving Henson agreed.

In 1891 Henson and Peary embarked on the first of seven Arctic expeditions they would make together. Henson quickly became a skilled dogsled driver and hunter, and he also learned the language and customs of the native Inuits. Peary found his abilities so valuable in the harsh, frozen land that he remarked, "I can't get along without him." On their last trip, the two men, accompanied by four Inuit, left the rest of the crew behind and made a dash for the Pole. Henson got there first, which he later recalled made Peary "hopping mad." From that time on, the commander scarcely spoke to him.

The feat brought Peary, the leader of the expedition, worldwide acclaim. However, it took decades—and changing racial attitudes—for Matthew Henson to receive the recognition he deserved for his contributions to Arctic exploration.

Matthew Henson played a key role in Robert E. Peary's successful expedition to the North Pole in 1909. In 2000 the National Geographic Society posthumously awarded Henson its highest honor, the Hubbard Medal (above), "for distinction in exploration, discovery, and research." The Society noted, "Henson embodies what this award stands for."

W. E. B. Du Bois

BORN February 23, 1868, Great Barrington, Massachusetts

DIED August 27, 1963, Accra, Ghana

AGE AT DEATH 95

OTHER NAMES William Edward Burghardt Du Bois—do BOYS—(birth name)

FAMILY Mother: Mary Burghardt Du Bois. Father: Alfred Du Bois. Married Nina Gomer in 1896, and they had two children. His son, Burghardt, died from dysentery in 1899. After his first wife died in 1950, Du Bois married Shirley Lola Graham.

LANDMARKS Boyhood homesite, Great Barrington, Massachusetts, a national historic landmark

MILESTONES 1895: Received Ph.D. from Harvard. 1903: *The Souls of Black Folk* published

HONORS Du Bois died on the eve of the 1963 March on Washington for civil rights. He was given a state funeral in Ghana.

Did You Know?

- In the 1950s, the U.S. government took Du Bois's passport away and persecuted him for his beliefs. He grew disillusioned with the slow pace of racial equality in the United States, and he joined the Communist Party. Near the end of his life he renounced his American citizenship and moved to the newly independent nation of Ghana in Africa.
- The death of Frederick Douglass (*see pages 72–75*) stirred Du Bois to dedicate his life to fighting for civil rights.
- In 1905 Du Bois helped found the Niagara Movement, which critiqued Booker T. Washington's views.
- Du Bois was accused of being an agent of a foreign power in 1951. The judge acquitted him of the charges.

AFRICAN-AMERICAN ACTIVIST William Edward Burghardt Du Bois grew up in Great Barrington, Massachusetts, where he was one of the few non-whites in town. During his college years at all-black Fisk University in Nashville, he became aware of the larger black culture—and of the harsh racism southern blacks endured. After Fisk, he went to Harvard University, and became the first African American to receive a Ph.D. from the prestigious school.

Du Bois, who went on to a long and distinguished career as a scholar and author, specialized in black history and in the emerging field of sociology (the study of human society). In 1903 he published a collection of essays called *The Souls of Black Folk,* in which he wrote: "The problem of the twentieth century is the problem of the color line." The book reflected the debate among black Americans about how to achieve racial equality.

One school of thought was led by influential educator Booker T. Washington. Washington urged blacks to get a practical education and make economic gains through hard work. This, he argued, would gradually earn them equal rights. In the meantime, he said, blacks should tolerate segregation and stay out of politics. Not surprisingly, many white leaders supported this approach.

Du Bois charged that Washington's way did nothing but perpetuate black disenfranchisement and oppression and discourage the higher education of black youth. African Americans deserved equal rights now, he said, and the best way to make this happen was through protest and political agitation. In 1909 he helped found the NAACP (National Association for the Advancement of Colored People), which quickly became the most effective force in America against racial injustice.

As the 20th century progressed, Washington's vision lost favor. Most African Americans came to agree with Du Bois that the best way to achieve social justice was by pushing for political equality.

W. E. B. Du Bois was a strong and eloquent voice in the movement for African-American rights. In The Souls of Black Folk, *he expressed his wish "to make it possible for a man to be both a Negro and an American, without being cursed and spit upon by his fellows, without having the doors of Opportunity closed roughly in his face."*

Mary McLeod Bethune

BORN	July 10, 1875, Mayesville, South Carolina
DIED	May 18, 1955, Daytona Beach, Florida
AGE AT DEATH	79
FAMILY	While Bethune came from a large family (she had 16 siblings), she only had one son.
LANDMARKS	Mary McLeod Bethune Council House, Washington, D.C. Grave on the grounds of Bethune-Cookman College, Daytona Beach, Florida
MILESTONES	1904: Founded the Daytona Educational and Industrial School for Negro Girls
HONORS	1935: NAACP Spingarn Medal. 1949: Haiti's highest medal of honor and merit

Did You Know?

- Bethune was good friends with Eleanor Roosevelt (*see pages 144–149*).
- The Bethune-Cookman College earned full accreditation under Bethune's leadership. Today the college enrolls 2,300 students.
- In 1939, Bethune took to the picket lines to protest discrimination in hiring practices for a drugstore chain.
- As early as 1942, she lobbied the U.S. War Department to commission black women officers. During World War II she also served as director of the Florida chapter of the American Red Cross.
- Bethune wrote a weekly newspaper column for the *Chicago Defender*.
- In her will, Bethune wrote, "Our children must never lose their zeal for building a better world. They must not be discouraged from aspiring toward greatness, for they are to be the leaders of tomorrow."

"THE DRUMS OF AFRICA BEAT IN MY HEART," Mary McLeod Bethune once said. "I cannot rest while there is a single Negro boy or girl lacking a chance to prove their worth." A dedicated educator, Bethune helped create a black women's movement and held a government post in the New Deal. Indeed, she accomplished so much in her lifetime that it is easy to believe she never did rest.

The daughter of former slaves, Mary McLeod was the 15th of 17 children. Her passion for education began when her parents chose her as the only one of their offspring to attend school. In return, she taught her siblings.

In 1904 Mary moved to Daytona, Florida, with her husband, Albertus Bethune, and their young son. Mary rented a run-down building, furnished it with crates and barrels, and opened a school for African-American girls. When she wasn't teaching, she was raising money. Her efforts paid off. In 1923 the school merged with a boy's school and became Bethune-Cookman College, with Mary Bethune as president. She also explored how black women could gain political power. In 1935 she founded the National Council of Negro Women, which eventually grew to 800,000 members.

Bethune's devotion to education brought her national recognition. In 1936 President Roosevelt appointed her director of the Office of Negro Affairs of the National Youth Administration (NYA). Under her leadership, almost 64,000 black students enrolled in NYA job-training programs. From 1940 until her death in 1955, tireless Mary McLeod Bethune also served as vice president for the NAACP.

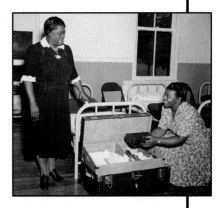

Mary McLeod Bethune quickly mastered the ways of Washington politics when President Roosevelt named her to his administration. One reporter noted, "Mrs. Bethune has gathered everything and everybody under her very ample wing." In World War II, Bethune served as assistant director of the Women's Army Corps. In the photo above, she greets an enlistee.

Helen Keller

BORN	June 27, 1880, Tuscumbia, Alabama
DIED	June 1, 1968, Westport, Connecticut
AGE AT DEATH	87
FAMILY	Father: Arthur Keller, who fought in the Confederate Army. Mother: Kate Adams. Two siblings: Phillips and Mildred
LANDMARKS	Helen Keller, Annie Sullivan, and Polly Thompson are all buried at the National Cathedral in Washington, D.C.
MILESTONES	1904: Graduated with honors from Radcliffe College
HONORS	1964: Presidential Medal of Freedom. Her autobiography, *The Story of My Life,* was named one of the top 100 books of the 20th century by the New York Public Library.

Did You Know?

- Anne Sullivan entered the Perkins Institution for the Blind in 1880, the year of Helen's birth.
- When Helen's dog, Lioness, was accidentally shot and killed in 1890, people pitched in to buy her a new dog. Helen gave the money to help a deaf-blind boy.
- Helen joined the Socialist Party in 1909 and remained active in socialist causes, especially fighting exploitation and oppression. Her beliefs caused her to oppose U.S. entry into World War I.
- In 1916 Helen became engaged to a man on her staff named Peter Fagan. Her mother forced them to break up. Bitterly disappointed, Helen later described her brief love as "a little island of joy surrounded by dark waters."
- Helen met every President from Grover Cleveland to John F. Kennedy.

HELEN KELLER COULD SEE AND HEAR until a few months before her second birthday. "Then," she recalled later, "came the illness which closed my eyes and ears and plunged me into the unconsciousness of a newborn baby." The illness, possibly scarlet fever, took away her sight and her hearing. But it did not destroy her spirit. Keller learned to communicate, and she lived life to the fullest. Her courage and determination still inspire people around the globe.

At first, Helen's parents took her to doctor after doctor in search of a cure for her blindness and deafness. None of them offered hope. Some even suggested that the Kellers put their daughter in an institution. But Helen's parents knew their little girl was too smart to be shut away. She used her own signs to communicate. If she wanted wanted a piece of bread, for example, she pretended to cut and butter a slice.

But Helen knew she was missing something. "Sometimes," she remembered, "I stood between two persons who were conversing and touched their lips. I could not understand....This made me so angry at times that I kicked and screamed until I was exhausted."

When Helen was six, her parents took her to Washington, D.C., to be examined by Alexander Graham Bell *(see pages 96–101)*, a leader in the field of deaf education. He recognized Helen's intelligence and advised the Kellers to contact the Perkins Institution for the Blind in Boston to find a teacher. The school recommended 20-year-old Annie Sullivan. Partly blind herself, Sullivan had learned how to communicate with deaf-blind people by using a hand alphabet to spell words into a person's palm.

Annie Sullivan arrived at the Kellers' farm in Alabama in

Blind and deaf from an early age, Helen Keller communicated by using a finger alphabet (above) to spell words into a person's palm. Her achievements made her an international symbol of triumph over physical handicaps. "When we do the best we can," she wrote, "we never know what miracle is wrought in our life, or in the life of another."

Frustrated by her world of silence and darkness, young Helen took comfort from her beloved dog (above left). She was six when teacher Annie Sullivan came into her life and taught her to sign words. Helen later referred to the day of Annie's arrival as her "soul's birthday." Annie, at right in the portrait above, remained with Helen until her own death in 1936.

March 1887. "The most important day I remember in all my life is the one on which my teacher came to me," Helen later wrote. Annie began spelling word after word into Helen's hand with her fingers. When she gave Helen a doll, for example, she spelled D-O-L-L into her palm. She wanted to teach Helen that everything has a name. In the meantime, she tried to help her wild pupil learn some self-control.

Helen's hand moves across a page of Braille. Learning to read Braille opened the world of the written word to her.

One day Annie held one of Helen's hands under a water pump. "As the cool stream gushed over one hand," Helen wrote later, "she spelled into the other the word water....Suddenly I felt a misty consciousness as of something forgotten...and somehow the mystery of language was revealed to me." By the end of the day Helen had learned a great many more words. Among them was T-E-A-C-H-E-R, which is what she called Annie Sullivan. The two of them would stay together for the next 50 years.

Helen learned with astonishing speed. When she was eight she and Annie went to the Perkins Institute. Helen learned to read Braille—a kind of writing that uses raised dots to represent letters and numbers. She began devouring books. At age 14 she entered a school for the deaf in New York. She learned to speak there, although her speech was never clear.

In 1900 Helen entered Radcliffe College, with Annie Sullivan at her side. During classes,

Annie spelled the professor's lecture into Helen's hand. Helen graduated with honors in 1904. While she was in college she wrote her autobiography, *The Story of My Life*. It became an international best seller and remains in print today.

After college, Helen earned a living by writing more books and articles about her life. She and Annie also went on lecture tours together. Over the years, Helen had become internationally famous as word spread of her amazing success. But Helen wanted more than fame. She wanted to help others, especially people who were blind. She began raising funds for the American Foundation for the Blind, work that eventually took her around the world several times. She persuaded Congress to fund programs for the blind. She also supported woman suffrage, workers' rights, socialism, and pacifism.

Helen learned to understand people's speech by "reading" their lips with her fingers. Here she "listens" to Grace Coolidge, the wife of President Coolidge.

Eager to experience everything life had to offer, Helen also made time for fun. She learned to ride a bicycle, to swim, and to ride horseback. She went to concerts and danced to the vibrations of the music. She charmed everyone she met, from emperors to scientists to actors to presidents, with her sense of humor and adventurous spirit.

In 1936 Helen's beloved Teacher died. Helen was devastated, but she was determined to keep working for the causes she believed in. Polly Thomson, Helen's secretary since 1914, became her new translator and companion. During World War II, Helen visited soldiers who had been blinded or made deaf in battle. She gave them hope that they could still live a happy and useful life. She died in 1968 at the age of 87.

"The mystery of language was revealed to me. I knew then that 'w-a-t-e-r' meant the wonderful cool something that was flowing over my hand. That living word awakened my soul, gave it light, hope, joy, set it free!"

The Story of My Life, 1902

The story of Helen Keller and Annie Sullivan's first months together inspired a 1956 television drama called "The Miracle Worker." It was later made into a play, and then an award-winning movie. Patty Duke, the actress who portrayed young Helen in the film, visited 81-year-old Helen and spoke with her by signing.

Alice Paul

Did You Know?

- Founded in 1984, the Alice Paul Institute is a not-for-profit organization that is based out of her childhood home, Paulsdale, in Mount Laurel, New Jersey. It offers leadership and women's history workshops for eighth-grade girls.
- The Association of Women Faculty & Administrators at the University of Pennsylvania sponsors the Alice Paul Award. It is given each April to women faculty and students who have made distinguished contributions to life for women at the university.
- In 2004, HBO produced *Iron Jawed Angels* starring Hilary Swank, a film about Alice Paul and the National Women's Party.

"How is it," Alice Paul wondered in 1917, "that people fail to see our fight as part of the great American struggle for democracy?" She referred to the fight for women's voting rights, or suffrage, a cause for which she repeatedly risked her own freedom.

Alice Paul grew up in New Jersey. After graduating from college in 1905, she studied in England. She threw herself into the British suffrage movement, joining women in their defiant demonstrations to demand the vote. Her efforts landed her three jail terms.

When she returned home to the United States, Paul became a leader in the fight for American women's votes. In 1913 she helped organize a massive woman-suffrage parade, in which some 8,000 women marched through Washington, D.C. When President Woodrow Wilson refused over the years to support a woman suffrage amendment, Paul turned to a new tactic: In 1917 she and her followers began picketing the White House, carrying banners that asked such things as, "How long must women wait for liberty?" Before long, police were arresting the picketers. Alice Paul was sentenced to seven months in prison. When she went on a hunger strike to protest being a political prisoner, she was force-fed.

News of the mistreatment Paul and other suffragists received in jail outraged the public. In 1918 Wilson finally announced his support for woman suffrage. In 1920 the 19th Amendment to the Constitution was ratified. Thanks in great part to Alice Paul, who finished the fight begun by Elizabeth Cady Stanton and others *(see pages 76–81)* in 1848, American women finally had the vote.

Suffragist leader Alice Paul (left) toasts ratification of the 19th Amendment, which gave women the vote, in August 1920. Paul stitched the stars on the banner behind her to keep count of state ratification votes. The suffrage parade she helped organize in 1913 (above) brought national attention to the cause of women's voting rights.

Charles Lindbergh

★

BORN	February 4, 1902, Detroit, Michigan
DIED	August 26, 1974, Maui, Hawaii
AGE AT DEATH	72
FAMILY	Father: Charles August Lindbergh, a lawyer and congressman. Mother: Evangeline Lodge Land, a science teacher. Lindbergh married Anne Spencer Morrow in 1929. They had six children.
LANDMARKS	Charles A. Lindbergh Historic Site, Little Falls, Minnesota
MILESTONES	May 20–21, 1927: First nonstop New York-to-Paris flight
HONORS	1927: Congressional Medal of Honor. The Minneapolis/St. Paul International Airport has a terminal named for him. The San Diego International Airport-Lindbergh Field also honors him.

Did You Know?

- The *Spirit of St. Louis* was only 27 ¹/₂ feet long and 9 feet 10 inches high. Its wingspan was 46 feet.
- Before Lindbergh's successful transatlantic flight, six men had died in earlier attempts at the feat.
- Lindbergh's grandson, Erik Lindbergh, duplicated his grandfather's transatlantic feat 75 years later, in 2002.
- Lindbergh's book about his famous flight won the Pulitzer Prize in 1953.
- In the 1960s Lindbergh spoke in favor of protection of whales. He was also influential in establishing protections for an indigenous Filipino group, the Tasaday.
- President Dwight D. Eisenhower named Lindbergh a brigadier general in the Air Force Reserve in 1954.

IN MAY 1927, CHARLES LINDBERGH FLEW NONSTOP from New York to Paris in a small silver plane called the *Spirit of St. Louis*. Just 25 years old, Lindbergh was the first person ever to make the transatlantic flight. The courageous feat thrilled people around the world. And it turned the tall, handsome, boyish-looking Lindbergh into America's most popular hero ever.

Growing up, Charles lived half the year on his family's farm in Minnesota and the other half in Washington, D.C., where his father was a U.S. congressman. During World War I, Charles dreamed of becoming a fighter pilot, but the war ended before he was old enough to enlist. After high school he enrolled at the University of Wisconsin. He soon decided college life was not for him. What he really wanted to do was fly. He talked his parents into letting him go to a flying school in Nebraska.

In 1923 Lindbergh bought a surplus army training plane. Billed as "Daredevil Lindbergh," he took off on a stunt-flying tour through the South and Midwest. He enlisted in the Army Air Service in 1924 to learn how to fly newer, more powerful planes. In 1926 he took a job as an airmail pilot.

Now that he had achieved his dream of becoming a pilot, Lindbergh itched for a new challenge. As he later explained, "I had been attracted to aviation by its adventure, not its safety, by the love of wind and height and wings." He decided to compete for the $25,000 prize being offered for the first nonstop flight between New York and Paris. He persuaded a group of businessmen in St. Louis to finance his venture, then had a new, single-engine plane built to his specifications. In the

Named the first ever "Man of the Year" by Time *magazine (above), Charles Lindbergh captivated the world when he made the first nonstop flight from New York to Paris in May 1927. His plane, the* Spirit of St. Louis *(left), now hangs in the Smithsonian's National Air and Space Museum in Washington, D.C.*

About a week after his historic landing in Paris, Lindbergh flew the Spirit of St. Louis *to Belgium, where he received another rousing welcome (above left). When he returned to the United States, more than three million people turned out to cheer the young hero as he rode in a ticker-tape parade up Broadway in New York City.*

meantime he hoped that none of the other pilots going after the prize would beat him to it.

On May 20, 1927, Lindbergh squeezed into the cramped cockpit of the *Spirit of St. Louis* and took off from Roosevelt Field, New York. Fighting sleepiness much of the way, he flew 3,600 miles through clouds, fog, ice, and storms. When he neared Ireland, he flew close to some fishing boats to ask if he was headed the right way. Finally, after 33 ½ hours in the air, he landed in Paris.

A huge and cheering crowd greeted Charles Lindbergh at the landing strip. Around the world, radio announcers broadcast the news of his successful flight, and the shy aviator became an instant celebrity. Reporters clamored for interviews with him.

Back in the United States, Lindbergh received a hero's welcome in town after town. He toured the country in the *Spirit of St. Louis* to promote aviation. He also made a goodwill flight to Mexico. While he was there he met the U.S. ambassador's daughter, Anne Morrow. They married in 1929. Anne learned to fly and navigate, and over the years she and Charles traveled all over the world together, exploring new air routes and mapping them for the emerging airline industry.

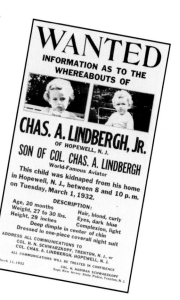

Charles and Anne Morrow Lindbergh traveled the world together as aviation pioneers. Tragedy struck in 1932, when their infant son was snatched from his crib. A massive search for the child ensued, with posters distributed across the country (right). He was later found murdered. The Lindberghs believed the excessive media attention they received contributed to the kidnapping of their son.

> "I saw a fleet
> of fishing boats....
> I saw some men and flew down
> almost touching the craft
> and yelled at them,
> asking if
> I was on the right road
> to Ireland....
> An hour later
> I saw land."
>
> "Lindbergh's Own Story,"
> *New York Times,* May 23, 1927

Lindbergh soars over the Eiffel Tower in the Spirit of St. Louis. *He believed that his flight from New York to Paris was "the forerunner of a great air service from America to France, America to Europe, to bring our peoples nearer together in understanding and in friendship than they have ever been."*

In 1932 the Lindberghs' first child, a son named Charles, was kidnapped from his crib in their New Jersey home and murdered. The media's sensational coverage of the crime and the trial of the kidnapper disgusted the Lindberghs. In 1935 they moved to England with their second son to protect their family and escape the constant hounding by the press.

While in Europe, Lindbergh visited German aviation centers. He was both impressed and alarmed by the growing air power of Nazi Germany. On one trip he was given a medal by his Nazi hosts. His acceptance of it shocked many people in America. The Lindberghs returned to the United States in 1939, just before World War II broke out in Europe. Lindbergh began speaking out against American involvement in the war. In one controversial speech he identified "the British, the Jewish, and the Roosevelt Administration" as pressing the country toward war. Public statements like this, along with his relations with the Nazis, disillusioned many of his former admirers. Some Americans even saw him as a traitor.

But when the United States entered the war in 1941, Lindbergh committed himself to the war effort. He served as a civilian consultant to fighter pilots in the Pacific, and he flew 50 combat missions himself.

After the war, Lindbergh flew around the world in support of efforts to preserve endangered species and wild places. He continued flying until shortly before his death, at the age of 72.

Today Charles Lindbergh is regarded as one of America's most controversial heroes. His reputation never recovered from the charges that he was anti-Jewish and a Nazi sympathizer. But he deserves to be remembered for his heroic solo flight from New York to Paris in 1927 and his many contributions to aviation.

Amelia Earhart

BORN	July 24, 1897, Atchison, Kansas
DIED	(Disappeared) July 2, 1937, near Howland Island, central Pacific Ocean
AGE AT DEATH	39
OTHER NAMES	Lady Lindy
FAMILY	Earhart had one sister, Muriel. Amelia married George Palmer Putnam in 1931.
LANDMARKS	The house where she was born in Atchison, Kansas, is now a museum. Amelia Earhart Memorial Bridge, Atchison, Kansas
MILESTONES	May 20–21, 1932: Solo flight across the Atlantic; this flight took 14 hours and 54 minutes.
HONORS	1932: U.S. Air Force Distinguished Flying Cross and National Geographic Society's Special Gold Medal

Did You Know?

- When Amelia attended the 1908 Iowa State Fair, she thought that the airplane she saw was, "a thing of rusty wire and wood and not at all interesting."
- Earhart was not the only person in her family to have a "first." Her mother was the first woman to climb Colorado's Pike's Peak.
- Earhart encouraged women pilots to fly in a race from Los Angeles to Cleveland in 1929. The race was nicknamed the "Powder-Puff Derby."
- When Earhart vanished without a trace, a search team including 65 airplanes and 10 ships covered an area the size of Texas looking for her and her copilot.
- It wasn't until 1964 that a woman—two American women flying independently—circumnavigated the globe. They were Geraldine Mock and Joan Merriam Smith.

IN 1928, AMELIA EARHART CAUSED A SENSATION when she became the first woman ever to fly across the Atlantic Ocean. She became famous overnight for her daring and courage, even though she only rode as a passenger. In the early days of aviation, people were astounded that a woman was brave enough to go along at all on such a dangerous adventure. But that was just the beginning of Amelia Earhart's airborne adventures.

As a child growing up in Kansas, Amelia loved to look at maps and take make-believe journeys in an old carriage in her grandparents' barn. She saw a plane fly for the first time in 1908, when her father took the family to the Iowa State Fair to celebrate her 11th birthday. The Wright brothers (*see pages 106–109*) had made the first powered flight just five years earlier.

In December 1917, at the height of World War I, 20-year-old Amelia visited Toronto, Canada. She was deeply moved to see so many wounded soldiers, who had returned from fighting in Europe. For the rest of the war, Amelia worked as a nurse's aid at a military hospital in Toronto. She became friendly with some of the wounded pilots there. On her day off, she sometimes visited a nearby airfield to watch the pilots practice flying.

When the war ended, Amelia returned to the United States and enrolled at Columbia University in New York City as a premedical student. After a year, however, she left to join her parents, who were living in Los Angeles. She and

Amelia Earhart, shown here in the photograph from her pilot's license, made history in May 1932 when she become the first woman to fly solo across the Atlantic Ocean. As reflected in the editorial cartoon above, the American public was enthralled by her daring adventure, which received major press coverage.

Earhart's transatlantic flight ended in a pasture in Londonderry, Northern Ireland. From there Earhart flew on to the Hanworth Aerodrome near London (above). A crowd of well-wishers and journalists welcomed her, along with the U.S. ambassador to Britain.

her father often went to air circuses, a popular weekend entertainment, and her interest in aviation grew. In 1920, Amelia's first ride in an airplane thrilled her. She recalled, "As soon as we left the ground, I knew I myself had to fly."

Amelia worked odd jobs to pay for flying lessons. She borrowed money from her mother and bought her own plane, a small two-seater. After receiving her pilot's license, she began flying in exhibitions. In October 1922, she set a women's altitude record of 14,000 feet, and in May 1923, she earned her international pilot's license.

Amelia decided that a medical career was not for her. She moved to Boston, where she found a job as a social worker at a community center for immigrant children. She enjoyed her work with children, but

Amelia Earhart's record-breaking solo flight made her world famous. Here she visits with another celebrity— Hollywood movie star Cary Grant.

her passion for flying couldn't be denied. She continued to take to the air whenever she could.

In April 1928, Amelia received the telephone call that would make her famous. It was an offer to become the first woman to fly across the Atlantic Ocean. Two months later Amelia and two male pilots took off from Newfoundland, Canada, in a plane called the *Friendship*. It landed 20 hours and 40 minutes later near Burry Port, Wales. Astounded by all the attention she received merely for being a passenger, Amelia hoped to someday pilot a transatlantic flight herself. She wanted "to prove that I deserved at least a small fraction of the nice things said about me."

Amelia's life now revolved around flying, and she made one "first" after

> ## "Please know I am quite aware of the hazards.
> I want to do it because I want to do it.
> Women must try to do things as men have tried.
> When they fail, failure must be but a challenge to others."
>
> Letter to George Putnam, 1935

another. In October 1928, she became the first woman to make a round-trip solo flight across the United States. She competed in the first Women's Air Derby in 1929. In 1930, she set three women's world speed records. By 1932, Amelia was ready to cross the Atlantic again—this time as the first woman to make the flight alone. Braving violent thunderstorms and heavy fog for much of the journey, Amelia flew from Newfoundland to Ireland in record time.

Amelia's solo Atlantic flight earned her the respect of fellow pilots and the admiration of people around the world. She received many awards for her courage and skill, and she was in demand as a public speaker. On her lecture tours, she promoted the role of women in aviation. She also spoke out in support of women's rights and pacifism.

A few years later, Amelia embarked on her most ambitious voyage ever. On May 21, 1937, she and her copilot, Fred Noonan, took off from California on the first leg of a 29,000-mile journey around the globe. If successful, Amelia would achieve another first for a woman. Some six weeks and 22,000 miles later, Amelia and Fred landed in Lae, New Guinea. From there they set out for tiny Howland Island in the middle of the Pacific Ocean. Along the way, however, they lost radio contact, and they were never heard from again. A massive sea and air search failed to find any trace of the plane or its crew. Amelia Earhart's accomplishments live on, inspiring generations of girls and women to believe in themselves and work toward their dreams.

In May 1937 Amelia Earhart (perched here atop an autogiro, a predecessor to the helicopter) took off to circle the globe. Her plane's disappearance in the Pacific Ocean two months later made headlines (left) around the world.

Franklin Delano Roosevelt

BORN	January 30, 1882, Hyde Park, New York
DIED	April 12, 1945, Warm Springs, Georgia
AGE AT DEATH	63
OTHER NAMES	FDR
FAMILY	Married Anna Eleanor Roosevelt in 1905. They had six children, but a son died in infancy.
LANDMARKS	Franklin D. Roosevelt National Historic Site, Hyde Park, New York. Little White House State Historic Site, Warm Springs, Georgia. FDR Memorial, Washington, D.C. Campobello International Park, Campobello, Canada
MILESTONES	1933–1945: 32nd President of the United States
HONORS	The Franklin Delano Roosevelt International Disability Award recognizes nations that have made progress toward the goals of expanding opportunities for people with disabilities.

Did You Know?

- The country was suffering when FDR came to office, and one out of every four people was without a job.
- After Roosevelt won four terms in office, many Americans felt that there needed to be a limit on how many times someone could be elected President. In 1951, the 22nd Amendment limited Presidents to two terms.
- While FDR was stricken with polio in 1921, it wasn't until 1952 that the epidemic reached its peak in the United States. In 1952, 58,000 Americans were infected.
- During his presidency, a majority of African Americans supported FDR—dropping their historic allegiance to the Republican Party.

FRANKLIN DELANO ROOSEVELT SERVED the longest Presidency in United States history. During his 12 years in office he lifted the nation out of the Great Depression and then guided it safely through the worst days of World War II. Roosevelt knew how high the stakes were. "We are fighting," he said in 1936, "to save a great and precious form of government for ourselves and for the world." His heroic leadership helped America survive these two crises.

Born at his wealthy family's estate in Hyde Park, New York, Franklin was an only child. His parents, James Roosevelt and Sara Delano Roosevelt, had him tutored at home until he was 14. After graduating from Harvard in 1904, Franklin attended Columbia Law School. Then he went to work for a New York law firm.

In the meantime, Franklin fell in love with a distant cousin, Eleanor Roosevelt (see pages 144–149). They married in 1905. At their wedding, the bride was given away by her uncle, Theodore Roosevelt (T.R.), the President of the United States (see pages 110–111).

Franklin greatly admired T.R., and he followed in his footsteps by entering politics. In 1910 he was elected to the New York Senate. Unlike the Republican T.R., however, Franklin Roosevelt ran as a Democrat—perhaps because the ambitious young man saw more opportunities for himself in that party. A few years later Roosevelt was appointed assistant secretary of the Navy by President Woodrow Wilson. He held the post for about seven years, gaining experience that would help prepare him for his future role as a wartime leader. In 1920 Roosevelt ran as the Democratic nominee for U.S. Vice President.

Although the Democrats lost that election, Roosevelt gained a

During his first presidential campaign in 1932, Franklin Delano Roosevelt took great joy in meeting citizens across the country, including this young patient in Seattle (left). As President, he took an activist approach to ending the Great Depression that many people credited with saving the nation—a sentiment reflected in the campaign button above.

> "The test of our progress is not whether we add more
> to the abundance of those who have much;
> it is whether we provide enough for those who have too little."

Second Inaugural Address, January 20, 1937

lot of national attention, and his political prospects looked bright. In the summer of 1921, however, Roosevelt's life changed drastically when he was stricken suddenly with polio. The disease stole his physical strength and left his legs paralyzed. Eleanor encouraged him to fight for his recovery. Meanwhile she helped keep his career alive by attending political events on his behalf.

After three years of painful physical therapy, Roosevelt learned to stand on leg braces and to walk a few steps using crutches. He plunged back into politics, and in 1928 he was elected governor of New York. Four years later he ran for President of the United States.

By this time the nation was suffering from the worst economic crisis in its history, the Great Depression. One out of four workers was unemployed, banks across the country were failing, factories were closing, and farmers and families were losing their land and homes to foreclosures. In cities and towns across the country, the hungry and the homeless lined up at free soup kitchens for meals. Never before had life for so many in America seemed so hopeless.

So when the optimistic Roosevelt promised a "new deal for the American people," voters flocked to him. He overwhelmingly defeated the incumbent, Republican President Herbert Hoover, in the 1932 election. In his first Inaugural Address, Roosevelt declared, "The only thing we have to fear is fear itself." His words reassured his fellow citizens and brought them new hope.

As President, Roosevelt took bold action to end the Depression. In his first hundred days in office, he proposed and Congress passed a flurry of legislation. Among other things, these new laws restored faith in the banking industry; put people back to work building bridges, roads, dams, and power plants; aided farmers; and improved working conditions. Later measures regulated the stock market and created the Social Security system. These programs became known as the New Deal.

Roosevelt's New Deal helped many people get on their feet again, but he had many critics. Some were concerned that the New Deal gave the federal government too much power, and

After fighting his way back from polio, Franklin Delano Roosevelt refused to let his physical handicap limit him. Here, he steadies himself on the arm of a companion and throws out the opening pitch of the baseball season at Griffith Stadium in Washington, D.C. A huge baseball fan, Roosevelt encouraged the baseball commissioner to keep the baseball season going in 1942, even though many players were entering military service now that America was at war.

Although he was born into an extremely wealthy and powerful family, Roosevelt believed in and fought for the common person. During the Depression he talked with farmers in Georgia to see how they were coping (above left). During World War II, he visited troops stationed in Europe (above right). Ordinary citizens believed Roosevelt truly cared about them, and they elected him to four terms.

many of the rich—who called Roosevelt a "traitor to his class"—resented him for reducing their power and income. But most ordinary citizens, many of whom saw their lives improve, trusted Roosevelt so much that they elected him to three more terms.

When World War II broke out in Europe in 1939, Roosevelt saw the evil threat the Nazis posed to democratic nations everywhere. He promised "all aid to the Allies short of war." After the Japanese bombed Pearl Harbor on December 7,

1941, America entered the war. As commander-in-chief of the nation's armed forces, Roosevelt took an active role in plotting military strategy and appointing key generals and admirals.

The strain of the war took a toll on Roosevelt's health. About a month before the Allied victory in Europe, President Franklin Delano Roosevelt died of a brain hemorrhage at his retreat in Warm Springs, Georgia. Americans everywhere mourned the brave man who had helped them pull through some of the nation's toughest challenges.

At left, President Roosevelt shares a lighthearted moment with British Prime Minister Winston Churchill (to his left) and Soviet leader Joseph Stalin (to his right). The three men met at Yalta, on the Black Sea, in February 1945 to discuss how to reshape Europe at war's end. Roosevelt, shown at right addressing a joint session of Congress, pushed for the creation of the United Nations.

WAR, PROSPERITY, AND SOCIAL CHANGE

★ *1941–Present* ★

T he Japanese bombing of Pearl Harbor, Hawaii, on December 7, 1941, marked the first time since the War of 1812 that the United States was attacked on its own soil. America entered World War II immediately afterward. Wartime industries put Americans back to work and stimulated the economy. By the time the war ended in 1945, the United States was more prosperous than ever. It was also a global leader.

1945

The computer age began when ENIAC, the first electronic digital computer, was introduced in 1945. It weighed 30 tons and took up 1,800 square feet of floor space.

1954

The Supreme Court ruled that "separate but equal" schools were unconstitutional and ordered that minority children be allowed to attend the same schools as whites.

1964–1973

Officially the first U.S. ground troops were sent to Vietnam in 1965 to prevent the communist takeover of South Vietnam. More than 58,000 Americans died in the war.

1981

President Ronald Reagan named Sandra Day O'Connor as the first woman ever to serve on the Supreme Court. In 1993 Ruth Bader Ginsburg joined her on the bench.

The 60 years since then have brought enormous change to America. In many ways we have moved toward a more democratic society, thanks in great part to the heroes of the civil rights movement of the 1950s and 1960s and to the feminist movement of the 1960s and 1970s. Today the United States has been described as a "rainbow nation," in which people of all races and ethnic groups have a voice—if not always an equal say—in shaping the nation's politics, culture, and society.

As American society has changed, so has America's role in world affairs. Following World War II, the United States and the Soviet Union became bitter enemies. The Soviets wanted to spread communism throughout the world, and

---

★

> *"We can never get civil rights in America until our human rights are first restored."*
>
> MALCOLM X, 1964

★

---

the United States was determined to stop them. The nuclear arms race between the two superpowers created a military standoff known as the Cold War.

The Cold War ended in 1989, when communist governments in Eastern Europe fell from power. The United States emerged as the world's richest and most powerful nation, and many Americans breathed a sigh of relief as the threat of nuclear destruction seemed to fade. But on September 11, 2001, America was once again attacked on its own soil, this time by Islamic terrorists who crashed planes into the World Trade Center and the Pentagon. In response, the American government launched a global war on terrorism, which continues to this day.

Albert Einstein

AMERICANS WELCOMED ALBERT EINSTEIN with great excitement when he paid his first visit to the United States in 1921. The German-born physicist's mind-boggling theories dazzled the public, even though very few people understood the science behind them. What everyone did know, thanks to all the press coverage, was that Einstein was the most extraordinary genius of their time—and perhaps of all time. Merely by thinking about it, he had come up with a totally new explanation for time and space and the way the universe works. For many admirers, that was reason enough to hail him as a hero. When he arrived in New York, thousands of fans greeted his ship, and thousands more cheered him as his motorcade passed through the streets.

One of Einstein's revolutionary scientific theories, called the general theory of relativity, had been verified by astronomers in the fall of 1919. Newspapers around the world spread the news. Einstein, at the time a professor at the University of Berlin in Germany, became a global celebrity practically overnight. Surprised by his fame, Einstein soon put it to good use. He sold pictures of himself to journalists, then sent the money to a charity that helped orphans from World War I, which had ended only a year earlier.

Einstein made his first mark on science in 1905, when he was working six days a week as a patent clerk in Bern, Switzerland, and pondering the mysteries of the universe in his spare time. Among other accomplishments that year, Einstein introduced what became the

As a youngster, Albert Einstein—shown above at age 14 with his sister and best friend, Maja—pored over books on science with "breathless attention." After his theory of relativity was verified in 1919, the superstar scientist traveled the world giving lectures (left).

most famous equation ever: $E=mc^2$. Simply put, the equation says that there is a huge amount of energy bound up in a tiny amount of mass. This concept eventually led other scientists to develop nuclear weapons.

Science was Einstein's passion, but he was also devoted to efforts for peace, freedom, and social justice. During World War I he spoke publicly against Germany's role in the war and in favor of pacifism—the view that war and violence are morally unacceptable ways of settling conflict. His views made many people in Germany, which ended up losing the war, distrust him. The fact that he was a Jew made some people trust him even less.

Einstein was not particularly religious. But as prejudice and hatred against Jews—known as anti-Semitism—increased in Germany in the years following World War I, he began to identify more closely with his Jewish roots and to support Jewish causes. The main purpose of his 1921 visit to America, for example, was to help raise money for the Hebrew University in Jerusalem, a school especially for Jewish students.

Over the next decade, Einstein continued to use his fame to help make the world a better place. He gave interviews and speeches and wrote articles on causes close to his heart: pacifism, peace, freedom, and human rights. And he watched in alarm as the Nazi party, which was violently anti-Jewish, gained power in Germany. At great personal risk, he spoke out strongly against the Nazis and their leader, Adolf Hitler. When Hitler took over the government in 1933, Einstein knew his life was in danger in Germany. That fall he and his wife emigrated to the United States, where Einstein had accepted a position at the Institute for Advanced Study in Princeton, New Jersey.

The American public gave Einstein a hero's welcome when he first visited the United States in 1921. In New York, cheering crowds lined the streets as his motorcade (right) drove to City Hall.

> "Concern for man himself and his fate
> must always form the chief interest of all technical endeavors...
> in order that the creations of our mind shall be
> a blessing and not a curse to mankind."
>
> Address at the California Institute of Technology, 1931

In the United States, Einstein continued to criticize the Nazis. He helped raise money for refugee children and helped found a group to resettle Jews and other refugees fleeing from Nazi terror.

In 1939, after learning from other physicists that German scientists might be developing an atomic bomb, Einstein coauthored a letter to President Franklin Roosevelt. In it he alerted Roosevelt to the threat and urged him to start an American nuclear weapons research program. Einstein was horrified, however, when the United States dropped atomic bombs on the Japanese cities of Hiroshima and Nagasaki in August 1945.

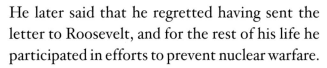

He later said that he regretted having sent the letter to Roosevelt, and for the rest of his life he participated in efforts to prevent nuclear warfare.

Einstein, who became an American citizen in 1940, loved and admired the United States. But he didn't hesitate to speak out against injustice in his new homeland. He condemned racial discrimination and supported the emerging African-American civil rights movement. And Einstein was one of the first public figures to criticize Senator Joseph McCarthy and his House Un-American Activities Committee when they began branding people as Communists and ruining their reputations and lives in the early 1950s. Einstein viewed McCarthy's investigations as a threat to intellectual freedom and to democracy itself. He publicly advised those called to appear before the committee to refuse to cooperate.

Einstein's passion for science lasted a lifetime. So did his commitment to humanity. At the end of his life, he signed a declaration urging all nations to give up nuclear weapons.

In 1921 Albert Einstein received the Nobel Prize for Physics and was awarded a gold medal, displayed front and back above. Over the next decade, he traveled the world giving lectures on science, peace, Zionism, and human rights. In 1931 Einstein spoke in Pasadena, California (left).

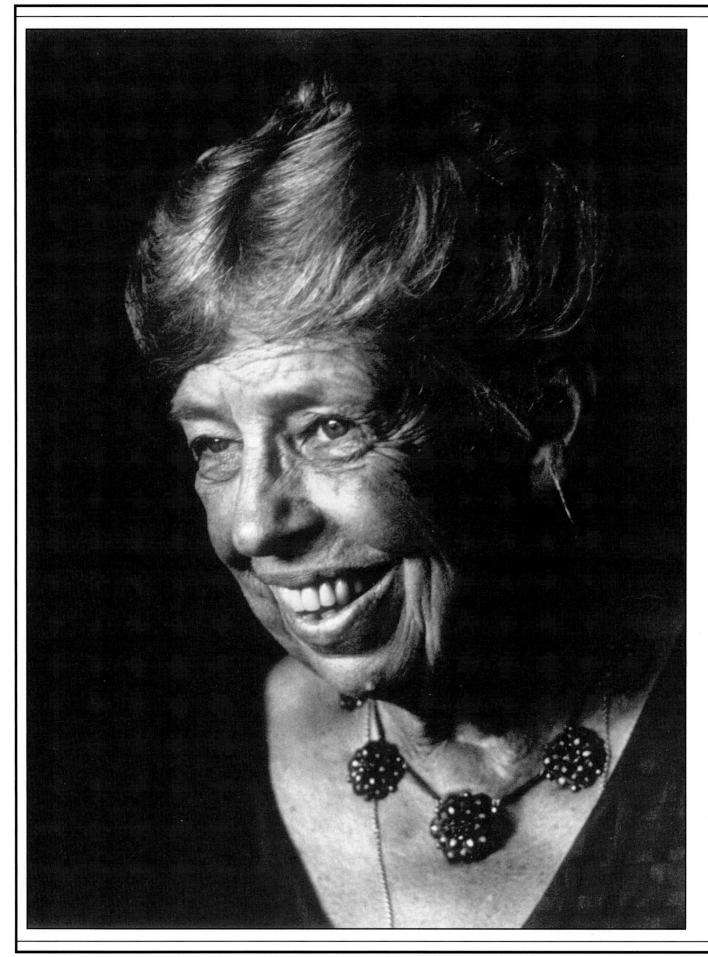

Eleanor Roosevelt

BORN October 11, 1884, New York, New York

DIED November 7, 1962, New York, New York

AGE AT DEATH 78

OTHER NAMES Anna Eleanor Roosevelt, "First Lady of the World"

FAMILY Married Franklin Delano Roosevelt in 1905. They had six children; one died in infancy.

LANDMARKS Eleanor Roosevelt National Historic Site, Hyde Park, New York. The site is the only historic site dedicated to a First Lady.

MILESTONES 1933–1945: First Lady. 1946: Appointed Chairman of the Commission on Human Rights at the United Nations

HONORS 1998: President Bill Clinton named an award for her work—the Eleanor Roosevelt Human Rights Award.

Did You Know?

- While acting as the "eyes and ears" for Franklin Roosevelt, she drove 38,000 miles during her first year as First Lady.
- During one of about 350 press conferences, she told reporters how to prepare a seven-cent lunch.
- She first started writing her syndicated column, "My Day," in 1935. By 1938 it appeared in 62 newspapers, six days a week.
- At a June 1947 Democratic fund-raising dinner in Los Angeles, California, she dined with a 31-year-old Frank Sinatra.
- Eleanor and Franklin Delano's marriage was often troubled, in part because FDR had an extramarital affair.
- Eleanor played an instrumental role in creating the United Nations General Assembly's Universal Declaration of Human Rights, in 1948.

BEFORE ELEANOR ROOSEVELT BECAME America's First Lady in 1933, the role of the President's wife consisted mainly of acting as the White House hostess. Eleanor soon changed that. She was committed to fighting poverty and racism and other injustices, and she used her position as First Lady to do just that. Along the way, she became one of the most admired and influential women of the 20th century.

Born Anna Eleanor Roosevelt to a wealthy, upper-class family in New York City, Eleanor was shy and insecure as a girl. Her beautiful mother, Anna Hall Roosevelt, was so disappointed in her daughter's lack of a pretty face that she called her "granny." Elliott Roosevelt, however, doted on his daughter, and Eleanor "never doubted that I stood first in his heart." Elliott's older brother, Theodore Roosevelt, was Eleanor's godfather.

When Eleanor was eight, her mother died from diphtheria. Elliott, an alcoholic, was deemed unfit to raise the children, so they were sent to live with their maternal grandmother. Grandmother Hall was a stern woman who believed that children needed strict discipline more than warm affection. Lonely Eleanor lived for her father's letters and visits. But when she was not yet ten, he died, too. Eleanor missed him very much. Looking back, she noted that as a child she "was always afraid of something; of the dark, of displeasing people, of failure." One thing that brought her comfort was helping others. She later recalled, "The feeling that I was useful was perhaps the greatest joy I experienced."

Overwhelmed by shyness as a girl (above), Eleanor Roosevelt later found she had a talent for public speaking. During her 12 years as First Lady, she greatly expanded the role of the President's wife. She traveled and gave speeches on her husband's behalf, and she also pursued her own causes, including civil rights.

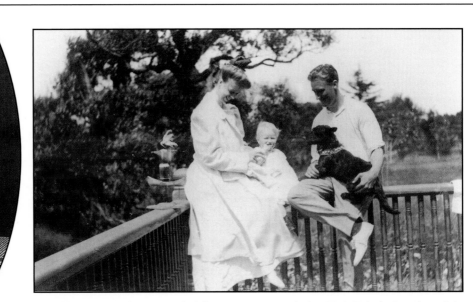

On her wedding day, Eleanor Roosevelt (left) was given away by her Uncle Ted, the President of the United States. At right, she and husband, Franklin, relax with their firstborn child, Anna, and dog, Duffy.

At age 15, Eleanor was sent to boarding school in England. In her three years at the school, which encouraged students to open their minds and think for themselves, she became less fearful and more confident and self-reliant. She felt that she was "starting a new life."

But when she was 18, her relatives called her back to America so that she could make her formal debut into New York society. Eleanor reluctantly returned. Still shy and self-conscious about her looks, she dreaded the round of parties and dances where young women were judged more for beauty than brains.

Eleanor wanted meaning in her life, and she soon found it by working to improve life for the poor. She taught dancing and exercise to children at a New York City settlement house, a shelter for newly arrived immigrants. She also joined a reform group called the Consumers' League, which investigated working conditions in garment factories and department stores. Eleanor was shocked by what she found. In one factory she "saw little children of four or five sitting at [work] tables until they dropped with fatigue."

During her social rounds, Eleanor became reacquainted with her distant cousin Franklin Delano Roosevelt *(see pages 134–137)*, whom she had known since childhood. He was drawn to her lively mind and compassion for others. She liked his confidence and cheerfulness. They married in 1905. At their wedding, Eleanor's Uncle Theodore, now President of the United States, gave the bride away.

After her marriage, Eleanor gave up her volunteer work. For the next ten years, she recalled, "I was always just getting over having a baby or about to have one, and so my occupations were considerably restricted during this period." In all, she had six children, one of whom died while he was still an infant.

While Eleanor was busy having babies, Franklin entered politics. He won a seat in the New York State Senate. A few years later he was appointed assistant secretary of the Navy, and the Roosevelts moved to Washington, D.C. When America entered World War I in 1917, Eleanor plunged back into volunteering. She served meals to servicemen at a Red Cross canteen several days a week, visited wounded soldiers in the hospital, and helped organize other services. She thrived on the challenge.

> "You gain strength, courage and confidence by every experience in which you really stop to look fear in the face.... You must do the thing you think you cannot do."
>
> *You Learn by Living*, 1960

In 1921, Franklin was stricken with a disease called polio, which paralyzed his legs. While he focused on regaining his health, Eleanor helped keep his political career alive. She attended Democratic Party functions on his behalf. She also traveled the country, acting as her husband's "eyes and ears" and reporting back to him on what she saw and heard.

Eleanor also devoted herself to causes close to her own heart. In the process she found she had a talent for organization and leadership. She helped head the League of Women Voters, founded after women won the right to vote in 1920. She also threw herself into efforts to end child labor, decrease the work week, and establish a fair minimum wage. Battling her natural shyness, she began speaking in public on politics and social reform and writing newspaper and magazine articles.

Franklin returned to public life in 1928, when he was elected governor of New York. Four years later, at the height of the Great Depression, he was elected President of the United States. Eleanor was happy for her husband, but she dreaded becoming First Lady. "As I saw it," she wrote, "this meant the end of any personal life of my own. I knew what traditionally should lie before me...and I cannot say that I was pleased at the prospect."

Rather than limit herself to traditional White House duties—including hostessing teas for 500 to 1,000 people in one afternoon—Eleanor quickly expanded the role of First Lady to include her own skills and interests. Just two days after Franklin's inauguration she held the first of what would become regular press conferences—the first President's wife ever to do so. Moreover, she restricted these sessions to female journalists. By doing so she hoped to motivate newspapers, which had mostly male staff at the time, to hire women reporters.

She took advantage of the publicity she received as First Lady to lobby for causes she embraced, such as the inclusion of women in

Eleanor Roosevelt was one of the most active—and most beloved—First Ladies in history. She not only joined her husband on the campaign trail (left), she crisscrossed the country to support his New Deal programs (center). During World War II, she traveled the globe to visit U.S. troops. In 1943 she paid a special visit to Seattle to pin a medal for bravery on Private Sam Morris (right).

After World War II, Eleanor Roosevelt traveled the world to promote international cooperation and peace. She delighted in making new friends. In New Zealand, she and a Maori woman rubbed noses—the traditional Maori greeting (above left). In 1946 President Truman appointed Eleanor a U.S. delegate to the new United Nations (above right). Delegates wear headphones to hear translations of speeches given in languages they do not understand.

politics and government, and she urged her husband to address issues she cared about. To reach out to Americans struggling to survive the Depression, Eleanor began giving radio talks. In 1935, she began writing a daily syndicated newspaper column called "My Day," in which she shared her opinions and experiences.

Eleanor again became the eyes and ears for her wheelchair-bound husband. Seemingly tireless, she flew all over the country, dropping in on city dwellers and country dwellers, farmers, coal miners, and factory workers. She wanted to see how people were coping and whether Franklin's New Deal programs were helping them. She spoke out on behalf of the poor and the powerless, and her concern and sympathy brought hope and comfort to millions

Eleanor Roosevelt's activism and Franklin Roosevelt's political talents made them a great team despite their often troubled marriage. Together they created lasting social and political change in America.

of Americans throughout the nation.

In her travels in the South, Eleanor witnessed racial discrimination firsthand, which inspired her to become an outspoken advocate of civil rights. She believed there could be no democracy in America as long as segregation and racism persisted. She noted, "We have poverty which enslaves and racial prejudice which does the same."

Eleanor practiced what she preached. In 1939, she attended a conference in Birmingham, Alabama, along with African-American educator Mary McLeod Bethune *(see pages 118-119)*. When told that a local segregation law prohibited her from sitting on the same side of the hall as her friend, Eleanor refused to sit on the white side. Instead, she had a chair placed for herself in the center. A few weeks later an outraged Eleanor publicly resigned her membership in the Daughters of the America Revolution when it refused to let the famous black singer Marian Anderson perform in its auditorium. She helped arrange for Anderson to sing a free concert on the steps of the Lincoln Memorial on Easter Sunday. More than 75,000 people attended the recital.

The nation had never seen a First Lady like Eleanor. Millions admired her, but some criticized her. Some people believed she was too outspoken and had too much influence over the President, who was elected to four terms. Others were enraged by her support for civil rights. But Eleanor continued to stand up for what she believed in. She said, "Everyone must live their own life in their own way and not according to anybody else's ideas."

During World War II, Eleanor traveled all over the world to visit U.S. troops. She also continued to speak out on civil rights. She pressed for equal opportunities for African Americans in the armed forces overseas and in factories and shipyards at home.

After Franklin Delano Roosevelt's death, Eleanor Roosevelt stayed very involved in politics. In July 1960 she addressed the Democratic National Convention in Los Angeles (above).

Eleanor was greatly saddened by Franklin Roosevelt's death in 1945, but she did not withdraw from public life. When President Harry Truman asked her to become a U.S. delegate for the new United Nations in 1946, she welcomed the chance to work for world peace. She chaired the U.N.'s Commission on Human Rights, and she helped write its Universal Declaration of Human Rights.

For the rest of her life, Eleanor stayed busy. She remained involved in politics and campaigned for her favorite candidates. She also continued to lecture, give radio broadcasts, and write about the causes she cared deeply about: racial justice, greater opportunities for women, and nuclear disarmament.

She delighted in visiting foreign countries, where she met with leaders and talked with ordinary people to learn about their customs and culture. In 1962, Eleanor Roosevelt died from tuberculosis at the age of 78. People everywhere paid tribute to the courageous woman who had become known as the "First Lady of the World."

"No one can make you
feel inferior without your consent."

This Is My Story, 1937

Margaret Mead

BORN	December 16, 1901, Philadelphia, Pennsylvania
DIED	November 15, 1978, New York, New York
AGE AT DEATH	76
FAMILY	Father: Edward Sherwood Mead, an economist. Mother: Emily Fogg, a sociologist. Mead was married three times. She had a daughter with her third husband, Gregory Bateson.
MILESTONES	1928: *Coming of Age in Samoa* published. 1929: Received her Ph.D. from Columbia University
HONORS	1975: Elected to the National Academy of Sciences, a prestigious organization of American scientists. 1979: Awarded the Presidential Medal of Freedom (posthumous)

Did You Know?

- Mead's ideas were controversial and often criticized. Mead hoped people would see that culture, instead of race, shaped human behavior.
- Mead popularized the term "generation gap" when she used it to describe differences between the experiences people had depending on if they were born before or after World War II. The term is still in use today to describe differences between older and younger people. Throughout her life, Mead was a great defender of young people.
- She wrote more than 1,000 articles.
- Mead was a curator at the American Museum of Natural History. Her office there was almost her home.
- Mead said, "Never doubt that a small group of thoughtful, committed citizens can change the world. Indeed, it is the only thing that ever has."

IN THE SUMMER OF 1925, 23-year-old anthropologist Margaret Mead set off on her own for the South Pacific islands of Samoa, 9,000 miles away from her hometown of Philadelphia. It was a big step for a young woman who "had never been aboard a ship...never spoken a foreign language, or stayed in a hotel by [herself]." But Mead's eagerness to jump into anthropological fieldwork outweighed any doubts she may have had.

Mead's goal was to observe and record the cultural behavior of Samoans living in remote villages. Little was known about these people, who still lived much the way their ancient ancestors had. Mead was determined to document their "unknown ways of life" before they vanished in the "onslaught of modern civilization." At the time anthropology was a fairly new science, so Mead had to invent some of her methods as she went along. She learned the native language and spent nine months living among the villagers.

When Mead returned to the United States, she took a job with the American Museum of Natural History in New York City. She also wrote a book about her pioneering work in Samoa. Published in 1928, *Coming of Age in Samoa* became a best seller. It introduced millions of Americans to anthropology and made Mead famous. It also shocked some people with its nonjudgmental observations of adolescent social life in Samoa, which was much "freer and easier and less complicated" than that of western teens.

Mead returned to the South Pacific several times to study other cultures. Later in life she studied American culture. She was particularly interested in gender roles. She used her celebrity to speak out on such topics as the Vietnam War, world hunger, and nuclear arms. But anthropology remained her passion. In her 1972 autobiography, she wrote, "I have spent most of my life studying the lives of other peoples—faraway peoples—so that Americans might better understand themselves."

Margaret Mead displays trophy heads she brought back after living among former headhunters and cannibals in New Guinea. Mead described her work as an "attempt to understand enough about culture so that all of us, equally members of humankind, can understand ourselves and take our future and the future of our descendants safely in our hands."

Rachel Carson

★

BORN	May 27, 1907, Springdale, Pennsylvania
DIED	April 14, 1964, Silver Spring, Maryland
AGE AT DEATH	56
FAMILY	Father: Robert Warden Carson, a salesman. Mother, Maria Carson, a teacher. Rachel never married.
LANDMARKS	Rachel Carson National Wildlife Refuge, Wells, Maine. The nearly 5,000 acres of the refuge, dedicated to Carson in 1970, are home to migratory birds and include freshwater wetlands and salt marsh.
MILESTONES	1962: *Silent Spring* published
HONORS	1951: National Book Award for *The Sea Around Us*. 1963: Named Conservationist of the Year by the National Wildlife Federation

Did You Know?

- Carson was ten years old when her first story was published in a children's literary magazine called *St. Nicholas.*
- The summer after Carson graduated from college in 1929, she went to Woods Hole Marine Biological Laboratory as a "beginning investigator." There were few women working there, and Carson felt isolated.
- Carson and her mother were very close. They lived together until her mother died in 1958.
- Carson combined her writing talent with her love of science to write articles about the Chesapeake Bay for the *Baltimore Sun* newspaper. She wrote under the name R.L. Carson, in the hopes that readers would think she was male and take her writing more seriously.
- The general use of the pesticide DDT in the U.S. was finally banned by the Environmental Protection Agency in 1972.

In her 1962 book, *Silent Spring,* biologist and writer Rachel Carson sounded an alarm: The reckless use of pesticides such as DDT and other toxic chemicals, she said, was poisoning the Earth and all its inhabitants. She accused the chemical industry and the U.S. government of encouraging the use of pesticides without knowing enough about their long-term effects. The book shook the nation.

Carson had been fascinated with "the beauty of the living world" since childhood. She majored in biology in college, then focused her graduate studies on marine life. From 1936 to 1952 she worked for the U.S. Fish and Wildlife Service. Meanwhile she combined her passion for science and nature with her desire to write. She wrote a trilogy of books about the sea, which sold so well that she was able to quit her job and write full-time.

In 1958 Carson received a letter from a woman who said that all the songbirds on her property died after a mosquito control plane sprayed pesticide over her town. The story inspired Carson to write a book about chemical pollution. For the next four years she collected data from scientists around the globe and documented the deadly effects of dangerous chemicals on living things. The result was *Silent Spring.*

The book quickly became a best seller. The powerful chemical companies attacked it as the work of a "hysterical woman," but independent investigations—including one ordered by President John F. Kennedy—soon supported Carson's conclusions. The public called for government regulation of pesticide use.

Rachel Carson's pioneering work helped launch the environmental protection movement in America. Her story shows the difference one person's voice can make in speaking out for change.

In Silent Spring, *Rachel Carson opened Americans' eyes to the dangers of pesticides, which came into widespread use after World War II. The book's title refers to the effect of the poisons on birds: "Over increasingly large areas of the United States...the early mornings are strangely silent where once they were filled with the beauty of bird song."*

Thurgood Marshall

BORN   July 2, 1908, Baltimore, Maryland

DIED   January 24, 1993, Bethesda, Maryland

AGE AT DEATH   84

OTHER NAMES   Thoroughgood Marshall (birth name), "Mr. Civil Rights"

FAMILY   Father: William Canfield Marshall, a waiter. Mother: Norma Arica Williams, a teacher. Married Vivian Burey in 1929. Married Cecilia Suyat in 1955 after his first wife died of lung cancer. They had two sons.

LANDMARKS   Thurgood Marshall Memorial, Annapolis, Maryland

MILESTONES   1967: First African-American Supreme Court justice

HONORS   2005: The Baltimore-Washington International Thurgood Marshall Airport was renamed in his honor. The Quinnipiac University School of Law offers The Thurgood Marshall Endowed Scholarship Award.

Did You Know?

- Marshall was made an honorary chief of the Kikuyu tribe in Kenya in 1961. He traveled to Kenya to help write the Kenyan constitution. He was particularly involved in the part of the constitution that protected the rights of the white minority there.
- Marshall argued the 1944 *Smith* v. *Allwright* case before the Supreme Court. He won and the Texas Democratic Party was forced to open up its primary and offer the ballot to 500,000 blacks in Texas. Other southern states were compelled to open up their primary voting, too.

A BRILLIANT LAWYER AND POWERFUL civil rights leader, Thurgood Marshall worked through the courts to end racial segregation and bring about equality for all Americans. In 1967 he became the nation's first African-American Supreme Court justice.

Marshall was born and raised in Baltimore, Maryland. His parents named him Thoroughgood after his great-grandfather, a freed slave who fought with the Union Army during the Civil War. As a young schoolboy, Thoroughgood got tired of writing out his long first name and shortened it to Thurgood. Thurgood grew up in a middle-class neighborhood. His father, William, was a waiter, and his mother, Norma, taught at an all-black elementary school.

Thurgood's father influenced him greatly. "He never told me to become a lawyer, but he turned me into one," Marshall later explained. "He did it by teaching me to argue, by challenging my logic on every point, by making me prove every statement I made." William Marshall also taught Thurgood and his brother to take pride in their race. In school, Thurgood sometimes argued with his teachers or joked around in class. For punishment, he had to memorize sections of the U.S. Constitution. By the time he graduated from high school, Marshall recalled, he knew the entire Constitution by heart.

Marshall attended Lincoln University—then an all-black college in Pennsylvania—and graduated with honors in 1930. He considered applying to law school at the University of Maryland but knew he would be rejected because he was black. Like countless other schools in the South

Known as "Mr. Civil Rights" during his years as a lawyer for the NAACP, Thurgood Marshall was our nation's first African-American Supreme Court justice—his official portrait is shown opposite. He served on the court for 24 years. Marshall and his second wife, Cecilia Suyat, had two sons: Thurgood Jr., and John (above).

Thurgood Marshall sits on the steps of the U.S. Supreme Court (left) with several members of the "Little Rock Nine"—the first black students to attend formerly all-white Central High School in Little Rock, Arkansas, in 1957. U.S. Army troops were called in to protect the students from racist mobs. Marshall, at center in the press conference at right, led the legal battle to outlaw segregation.

and other parts of America at that time, it was for whites only. Restaurants, hotels, parks, waiting rooms, drinking fountains, and hospitals were also segregated, or separated, by race. In the 1896 ruling known as *Plessy* v. *Ferguson,* the Supreme Court had ruled that "separate but equal" facilities for blacks and whites were legal. In reality, however, facilities for blacks were almost always inferior.

Marshall enrolled instead at Howard University Law School in Washington, D.C. His professors, several of whom were involved with the National Association for the Advancement of Colored People (NAACP), inspired him to use the law to fight segregation and discrimination. It would become his life's

As a lawyer for the NAACP, Marshall argued 32 cases before the Supreme Court. He won 29 of them.

work. He graduated first in his class, then opened his own law practice in Baltimore, where he became known for helping poor blacks. He also became active in that city's branch of the NAACP.

In 1935 Marshall took the case of a black man who wanted to attend the University of Maryland Law School—the same place that would not accept him. He based his arguments on the Constitution. "What is at stake here," he told the court, "is more than the rights of my client. It is the moral commitment stated in our country's creed." He won the case. The following year he joined the NAACP's national office in New York as a staff lawyer. A couple of years later he was made head lawyer of the organization.

> "In light of the sorry history of discrimination and its devastating impact on the lives of Negroes, bringing the Negro into the mainstream of American life should be a state interest of the highest order."
>
> Dissenting opinion,
> Bakke case, 1978

Marshall—shown here with his sons—was known in the Supreme Court for his sense of humor and his tart tongue. When he disagreed with a Court ruling, he often wrote angry dissents. He was especially disappointed with decisions against affirmative action—government policies that attempt to correct the effects of discrimination by increasing the proportion of minorities in jobs and educational institutions.

For the next two decades Thurgood Marshall traveled the country, leading the NAACP's legal battle to defeat racial segregation and extend equal rights to blacks. His greatest weapon was the Constitution, which he had memorized all those years ago. Insisting on the document's promise of equality, he fought against segregated schools, housing, restaurants, buses, and trains. He fought to change unjust laws that barred blacks from voting and serving on juries. This work took courage. He was threatened and harassed by local authorities in some southern towns, and he had to endure the very segregation he was trying to fight in some places.

As an NAACP lawyer, Marshall brought 32 cases before the Supreme Court. He won 29 of them, including *Brown* v. *Board of Education* of Topeka in 1954. In this groundbreaking case, Marshall challenged the concept of "separate but equal" schools for blacks and whites. "Equal," he argued, "means getting the same thing, at the same time, and in the same place." The court agreed. The justices declared unanimously that segregated schools were by their nature unequal, unjust, and unconstitutional. The decision transformed America.

In 1961 Marshall was named a judge on the U.S. Court of Appeals. In 1967 President Lyndon B. Johnson nominated him to the Supreme Court. He served as a justice for 24 years. During that time he remained a strong advocate for human rights. He fought against the death penalty, and he supported freedom of the press and privacy rights. Over the years, as other justices retired they were replaced by more conservative judges. As a result, the court began to draw back from affirmative action as a remedy for the damage done by legal discrimination. Marshall voiced his disappointment at this in angry dissenting opinions.

Thurgood Marshall retired from the Supreme Court in 1991. He died three years later. Historians agree that Marshall's successful efforts to outlaw segregation make him one of America's greatest civil rights leaders.

Rosa Parks

BORN   February 4, 1913, Tuskegee, Alabama

OTHER NAMES   "Mother of the Civil Rights Movement"

FAMILY   Married Raymond Parks in 1932. He died in 1977.

LANDMARKS   Rosa & Raymond Parks Institute for Self Development, Detroit, Michigan

HONORS   1979: NAACP Spingarn Medal. 1999: Congressional Gold Medal of Honor. Parks has an award named for her, the Rosa Parks Freedom Award, given by the Southern Christian Leadership Conference.

Did You Know?

- Parks was a seamstress and her husband a barber. They were both members of the NAACP.
- The bus laws in Montgomery, Alabama, stated that once blacks paid the driver their fare, they had to get off and get back on the bus using the back door. Two-thirds of the bus riders in Montgomery were African Americans.
- Parks's refusal to give up her seat gave the NAACP and Women's Political Council the chance to unleash an already planned and highly organized campaign.
- Parks's role in the bus boycott made it hard for her and her husband to find work in Montgomery, where they faced harassment by whites opposed to integration. In 1957 they moved to Detroit.
- Parks worked for Michigan congressman John Conyers, Jr. from 1965 to 1988.
- She and her husband established the Rosa and Raymond Parks Institute for Self Development, which helps young people train for careers.

On December 1, 1955, in Montgomery, Alabama, Rosa Parks boarded a city bus, paid her fare, and took a seat in the middle section. When some white passengers got on the bus at the next stop, the driver ordered the blacks onboard to give up their seats and move to the back. But Parks, a 42-year-old African-American seamstress and NAACP organizer on her way home, stayed put. With this simple act of courage, she triggered a chain of events that would jump-start the civil rights movement in America.

Parks knew she would be arrested for breaking the city's racial segregation laws, but as she later recalled, she "was tired of giving in." To protest Parks's arrest and the unjust law behind it, Montgomery's black residents, led by a young minister named Martin Luther King, Jr. *(see pages 172–177),* staged a boycott of the city's bus system. For more than a year, blacks walked or carpooled or took taxis instead of taking the bus. The bus company lost money, and Parks lost her job at the department store where she worked. But her case went all the way to the U.S. Supreme Court, which ruled in December 1956 that Montgomery's segregation policy was unconstitutional. Inspired by the success of the peaceful boycott, civil rights leaders relied on similar tactics as they challenged racial injustice throughout the South over the next decade.

Parks stayed active in the civil rights movement. She also supported the anti-apartheid movement in South Africa. Today Rosa Parks shines as an example of how one person can help change the world for the better by refusing to bow to injustice.

When Rosa Parks refused to give up her bus seat to a white passenger on a Montgomery, Alabama, bus in December 1955, she sparked a civil rights revolution. Later known as the "Mother of the Civil Rights Movement," Parks appeared with Jesse Jackson at the Democratic National Convention in 1988 (above).

Jonas Salk

Did You Know?

- More than 900 scientists and their assistants work at the Salk Institute, which was founded in 1960.
- Salk never patented the polio vaccine. He thought it would be easier to distribute around the world without a patent.
- Salk called war "the cancer of the world" and had hopes that one day this disease would be cured, too.
- The effectiveness of giving a live or a killed vaccine was a heated controversy early in the fight against polio. By 1961, Salk's vaccine had been replaced by a "live" virus vaccine created by Dr. Albert Sabin, Salk's rival. Sabin's vaccine was given by mouth, in a sugar cube. Scientists today know that Salk's vaccine was highly effective.
- Polio cases still occur. In 1988, the World Health Assembly passed a resolution to support an effort to wipe out the disease. That year there were 350,000 cases of polio. The latest figures show that there were fewer than 1,500 cases in 2004, but the disease appears to be on the rise again.

PEOPLE ACROSS AMERICA REJOICED in April 1955 when they heard the good news: Jonas Salk and a team of other scientists had developed a successful vaccine against the crippling disease called polio.

A highly contagious viral infection, polio struck without warning. It left many of its victims with paralyzed arms or legs. Some had to rely on machines to help them breathe, and many died. The number of polio cases in the United States soared in the 1940s and 1950s. Parents everywhere feared for their children. Conquering the dreaded disease made Salk a national hero.

Salk was born and raised in New York City. After completing medical school, he studied viruses at the University of Michigan. During World War II, he helped create an effective flu vaccine, which was eventually given to millions of soldiers.

In 1947 Salk set up his own lab at the University of Pittsburgh. Two years later he received funding from the Infantile Paralysis Foundation (now the March of Dimes) to develop a vaccine for polio. Other researchers raced for the same goal, but Salk and his colleagues got there first. Before testing the vaccine on nearly two million children, Salk injected himself and his family to make sure the new vaccine was safe. In 1955 the results were in: Salk's injected vaccine, which used deactivated, or "killed," viruses, was safe and effective. Children across the nation began receiving doses.

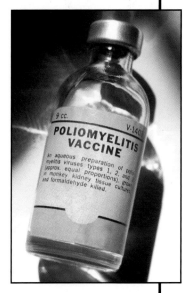

By the mid 1970s, the United States was polio free. Dr. Jonas Salk went on to research cancer and multiple sclerosis. A few years before his death in 1995, he began to search for a vaccine for AIDS.

Dr. Jonas Salk injected his polio vaccine (above) into himself and his family members before starting trials with a larger population. He explained, "You wouldn't do unto others that which you wouldn't do unto yourself." Salk was uncomfortable with all the publicity he received following the announcement of his successful vaccine.

Jackie Robinson

BORN January 31, 1919, Cairo, Georgia

DIED October 24, 1972, Stamford, Connecticut

AGE AT DEATH 53

OTHER NAMES Jack Roosevelt Robinson (full name)

FAMILY Wife: Rachel Isum. Three children: Jackie Jr., Sharon, David. Jackie Jr. died in 1971.

LANDMARKS National Baseball Hall of Fame, Cooperstown, New York

MILESTONES 1962: First African American inducted into the National Baseball Hall of Fame

HONORS 1947: National League (baseball) Rookie of the Year. 1949: Most Valuable Player award (National League) 1982: Congressional Medal of Freedom (posthumous)

Did You Know?

- Robinson played for the Kansas City Monarchs (Negro American League) and was number 42 for the Brooklyn Dodgers (National League). Robinson's lifetime batting average was .311. He led the National League in stolen bases in 1947 and 1949.
- Robinson ran a men's apparel store in New York's Harlem from 1952 to 1958.
- He appeared on a postage stamp in 1982.
- In 1970, he began the Jackie Robinson Construction Company to build housing for low-income families.
- Besides playing baseball, Robinson held a variety of jobs. He was a second lieutenant in the U.S. Army, a businessman, and a spokesperson for the NAACP.
- Throughout his life, Robinson was an advocate for civil rights. He remarked, "I won't 'have it made' until the most underprivileged Negro in Mississippi can live in equal dignity with anyone else in America."

ON APRIL 15, 1947, JACKIE ROBINSON stepped out of the Brooklyn Dodgers dugout at Ebbetts Field in Brooklyn and took his position at first base. With those steps, the 28-year-old African-American athlete broke the unwritten law that had kept blacks out of major league baseball for decades.

The grandson of a slave and the son of a sharecropper, Jackie was raised in Pasadena, California. During his college years at UCLA, he was an All-American running back on the football team. He also excelled at basketball, track, and baseball. After a stint in the Army, in 1944 Jackie signed on with the Kansas City Monarchs to play baseball in the Negro leagues—the only option open to African-American players at the time. Like many schools, restaurants, and other establishments in America in the 1940s, baseball was segregated by race.

While Jackie was with the Monarchs, he came to the attention of Branch Rickey, the president and general manager of the Brooklyn Dodgers. Rickey wanted to integrate major league baseball because he believed it was the right thing to do. He also thought it would be good for business. Talented black players could help him build a strong team that would win games and attract more fans to the box office.

When Rickey met Robinson and offered him the opportunity to play major league baseball, their meeting became the stuff of baseball legend. Playing the role of racist fans and

Jackie Robinson broke major league baseball's color barrier on April 15, 1947, when he played his first game with the Brooklyn Dodgers. He endured heckling and racial taunts— some from his own teammates—during his first years as a Dodger, but he soon became a favorite of many young fans, who eagerly collected Jackie Robinson baseball cards and comics (above).

players, Rickey shouted insult after insult at Jackie to test his patience. Finally Jackie burst out, "Mr. Rickey, are you looking for a Negro who is afraid to fight back?" Rickey snapped at him, "Robinson, I'm looking for a ballplayer with guts enough not to fight back."

Jackie was a proud man and a fierce competitor. It was not in his nature to take abuse without fighting back. When he was in the Army, for example, he risked court martial rather than move to the back of a military bus. But Jackie decided that breaking the color line and overcoming segregation were more important than his pride. He agreed to control his hot temper and not respond to racial attacks. He would take the lead in what came to be called the "Noble Experiment."

In Jackie's first season with the Brooklyn Dodgers, he earned new fans with every game. A daring base runner, he was also a great hitter and a skillful infielder. His bold style of baseball made him fun to watch. Branch Rickey described him as "all adventure on a ball field." Crowds—both black and white—flocked to see Jackie Robinson play.

At the end of the season, Jackie led the league in stolen bases. He was second in runs scored. To top things off, he was named the league's first

Young baseball fans were among Robinson's first supporters, and he enjoyed giving them his autograph. His talent and courage eventually helped make him a hero to countless Americans of all ages and colors.

ever Rookie of the Year.

But Jackie's success did not come easy. Some of his own teammates protested against having to play with an African American. They only gave in when Dodger management told them they could either play with Jackie or leave the team.

The problems with the Dodgers, however, were minor compared to what Jackie had to endure from others. Bigoted spectators threw bottles and screamed racial insults at him. Prejudiced members of opposing teams taunted him with hateful words. Pitchers threw the ball at his head on purpose, and runners deliberately dug their spikes into his shin when they slid into base. Hate mail and death threats were sent to Jackie and his family.

Somehow Jackie Robinson found the strength to hold his anger in check. He believed he was playing for all people of his race. Many of his African-American admirers, Jackie noted in his autobiography, "had not been baseball fans before I began to play in the big leagues. Suppressed and repressed for so many years, they needed a victorious black man as a symbol. It would help them believe in themselves." Gradually, other black ball players joined him in the major leagues.

"Plenty of times I wanted to haul off
when somebody insulted me for the color of my skin,
but I had to hold to myself. I knew I was kind of an experiment.
The whole thing was bigger than me."

Autobiography, *I Never Had it Made*, 1972

In Game One of the 1955 World Series against the New York Yankees, Jackie Robinson electrified fans when he stole home and slid under catcher Yogi Berra's glove. The umpire called him safe, although Berra felt he had nailed him. The Dodgers went on to win the series for the only time in Brooklyn history. Jackie Robinson stole home an incredible 19 times during his major league career.

Eventually, Jackie's tremendous talent, grace, and courage on and off the baseball field made him a hero to countless Americans of all colors.

After leading the Dodgers to six league championships and their first ever World Series victory, Jackie retired from baseball after the 1956 season. He turned his attention to business and the civil rights movement. In 1962 Jackie became the first African American inducted into the Baseball Hall of Fame. In honor of the occasion, President John F. Kennedy declared that Robinson "has demonstrated in his brilliant career that courage, talent and perseverance can overcome the forces of intolerance....The vigor and fierce competitive spirit that characterized his performance as an athlete are still evident in his efforts in the great battle to achieve equality of opportunity for all people."

The most touching tribute, however, came from Jackie's friend Dr. Martin Luther King, Jr. "Back in the days when integration wasn't fashionable," King said, Jackie Robinson "underwent the trauma and the humiliation and the loneliness which comes with being a pilgrim walking the lonesome byways toward the high road of Freedom. He was a sit-inner before sit-ins, a freedom rider before freedom rides. And that's why we honor him tonight." Jackie Robinson died in 1972. We still honor him today.

In 1962 Jackie Robinson became the first African American inducted into the Baseball Hall of Fame. The plaque he holds here now hangs in the Hall of Fame gallery in Cooperstown, New York.

John Glenn

Did You Know?

- The *Friendship 7* flight lasted 4 hours,
55 minutes. The distance flown was
75,679 miles.
- Shortly after his first flight into space,
Glenn was offered a million dollars by
the General Mills Company to appear
on the Wheaties cereal box. But Glenn
turned it down on principle—he
thought it would be wrong, as he
was still in the Marine Corps and still
an astronaut.
- Glenn ran for the U.S. Senate seat from
Ohio three times. He withdrew from
the race in 1964, lost in 1970, and won
in 1974.
- Glenn was a close friend of Robert
F. Kennedy and supported Senator
Kennedy in his 1968 run for the
presidency. He was later one of the pall-
bearers at Senator Kennedy's funeral.

HALF A CENTURY AGO, THE UNITED STATES and the nation then known as the Soviet Union began competing to see which country would be first to explore outer space. On April 12, 1961, the Soviets captured the lead when they launched the first person—cosmonaut Yuri Gagarin—into orbit around Earth. Ten months later the United States closed the gap in the space race when American astronaut John Glenn blasted off on February 20, 1962 aboard the *Friendship 7* and circled the Earth three times.

Glenn became a hero overnight for his brave voyage into the unknown. Parades in his honor were held across the country. Support for America's space program grew stronger than ever.

Glenn, who had served as a fighter pilot in World War II and Korea, left the space program in 1964. Ten years later voters from his home state of Ohio elected him to the United States Senate. He served four terms.

On October 29, 1998, John Glenn returned to space, this time as the oldest astronaut ever. On a nine-day mission aboard the space shuttle *Discovery,* 77-year-old Glenn acted as a human guinea pig for investigations into the aging process. His adventurous spirit made him a role model for Americans of all ages.

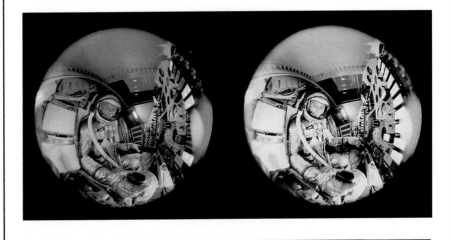

John Glenn practiced in simulations (above) to prepare for his pioneering mission on the Friendship 7 *spacecraft in 1962. He returned to space 36 years later. He said that he was "probably more nervous" the first time, because "in those days...we did not know much about spaceflight....We were sort of feeling our way and finding out what would happen to the human body in space...."*

Malcolm X

BORN	May 19, 1925, Omaha, Nebraska
DIED	February 21, 1965, New York, New York
AGE AT DEATH	39
OTHER NAMES	Malcolm Little (birth name), el-Hajj Malik el-Shabazz (Muslim name)
FAMILY	Married Betty X (Sanders), later known as Betty Shabazz, in 1958. They had six daughters.
LANDMARKS	The Audubon Ballroom, Harlem, New York, where Malcolm X gave his final speech, now contains a memorial mural.
MILESTONES	April 1964: Took part in the hajj, or pilgrimage, to Mecca

Did You Know?

- Malcolm X befriended an Olympic gold-medal-winning boxer named Cassius Clay. Now known as Muhammad Ali, the famous boxer rejected his birth name when he converted to Islam in 1964.
- As a teenager Malcolm wanted to be a lawyer, but he was discouraged when his teacher told him that this career was an unrealistic goal for a Negro.
- Malcolm founded the Organization of Afro-American Unity, a group that aimed to help put his ideas into action.
- Alex Haley helped to write his autobiography, *The Autobiography of Malcolm X*, which became a best seller in 1965.
- Malcolm X's philosophies and life continue to influence hip-hop and rap musicians. In 1992 Spike Lee directed *Malcolm X*, a film about the life of the black leader.

MALCOLM X BELIEVED THAT IF African Americans really wanted equality, they had to seize it, not wait for whites to give it to them. "The white man wants black men to stay immoral, unclean and ignorant," he declared. "As long as we stay in these conditions we will keep on begging him and he will control us. We never can win freedom and justice and equality until we are doing something for ourselves!" Fifty years ago this was a radical message, and many people—both white and black—feared and criticized Malcolm X because of it. But countless others were inspired by his bold vision of black pride and power.

One of America's most controversial African-American leaders, Malcolm X was born Malcolm Little in 1925. He spent most of his childhood in East Lansing, Michigan. His father, Earl Little, was a Baptist preacher who called for blacks to stand up for their rights. When Malcolm was six his father was found dead, apparently crushed by a streetcar. Although police called the death an accident, the Little family suspected that Earl had been murdered by white racists because of his outspokenness.

Louise Little had a hard time raising her eight children on her own. When Malcolm was 14 his mother was committed to a mental institution, and Malcolm and his brothers and sisters were split up and placed in foster homes. Despite these troubles, Malcolm excelled at school. But after eighth grade he quit school and moved to Boston to live with relatives. He soon drifted into a life of crime. Shortly before his 21st birthday he was convicted on a burglary charge and sentenced to ten years in prison.

Malcolm went into prison angry with himself and everything

Malcolm X urged African Americans to take pride in their race and to take control of their lives. Frustrated by America's slow path to racial equality, he believed that blacks should gain "freedom by any means necessary" to fight white oppression. Killed by assassins in 1965, Malcolm X was praised at his funeral service as "our shining black prince" (above).

In 1964 Malcolm X ran into Martin Luther King at the U.S. Capitol (above, left). Although he challenged King's nonviolent approach to achieving black equality, Malcolm respected the civil rights leader, and their meeting was cordial. The last year of his life, Malcolm, shown above with one of his six daughters, left the Nation of Islam and became an orthodox Muslim.

else. A new world opened up to him, however, when he began to use the prison library. He started reading everything he could get his hands on. He was especially interested in books about slavery and black history and culture.

Malcolm's life was further transformed when one of his brothers introduced him to the political and religious organization known as the Nation of Islam, also called the Black Muslims. The group's leader, Elijah Muhammad, taught that white people were devils who deliberately oppressed black people. He said that blacks had to separate themselves from white society in order to achieve political and economic success. Malcolm took these ideas to heart.

By the time he was paroled from prison in 1952, Malcolm had joined the Nation of Islam.

> "I'm for truth, no matter who tells it. I'm for justice, no matter who it is for or against....I'm for whoever and whatever benefits humanity as a whole."
>
> *The Autobiography of Malcolm X, 1965*

He also had a new name. Like many others in the organization, he replaced his "slave" last name with an X. Malcolm X became a minister in the Nation of Islam and was soon in great demand as a speaker. He organized new mosques across the country, and under his leadership membership in the Nation of Islam rose from about 400 to 10,000 people by 1960.

A fiery and charismatic speaker, Malcolm especially appealed to the masses of African Americans living in slums in northern cities. He knew what their problems were because he had experienced them himself, and he voiced their anger and frustration. He taught them about their African heritage and urged them to take pride in it, saying "We are black first and everything else second." Malcolm X also

After Malcolm X left the Nation of Islam, he received several death threats. On February 21, 1965, he was gunned down at a rally in Harlem (above left) and died a short time later. Along with slain civil rights leader Martin Luther King, Jr., Malcolm X remains a source of inspiration and pride to many Americans, as reflected in the 1986 rally shown at right.

challenged Martin Luther King, Jr.'s *(see pages 172–177)* philosophy of nonviolent resistance. "Concerning nonviolence," he said, "it is criminal to teach a man not to defend himself when he is the constant victim of brutal attacks." Malcolm X preached that blacks should demand equal rights and be willing to use "any means necessary" to obtain them.

Eventually relations between Malcolm X and Elijah Muhammad began to sour, in part because Muhammad resented Malcolm's growing popularity. In 1964, Malcolm X split with the Nation of Islam and formed his own group, the Muslim Mosque, Inc. Soon afterward he went on a pilgrimage to Mecca, Saudi Arabia, the holiest city in the Islamic faith. There he met and worshiped with Muslims of many colors from all over the

Symbol of the slain leader, a large "X" shares space with a political flyer on the facade of Harlem's Audubon Ballroom, site of Malcolm's assassination.

world. "We were all participating in the same ritual," he wrote, "displaying a spirit of unity and brotherhood that my experiences in America had led me to believe never could exist between the white and the non-white." The experience changed Malcolm's life. He rejected Muhammad's view that all white people were evil and moved away from the idea of black separatism. And he began to reach out to the civil rights movement, hoping to expand it into a human rights movement.

Malcolm X seemed to know he had little time to practice his new ideas. In an interview on February 19, 1965, he said, "It is a time for martyrs now, and if I am to be one, it will be for the cause of brotherhood." Two days later he was gunned down by assassins at a rally in New York City's Harlem neighborhood.

Martin Luther King, Jr.

BORN	January 15, 1929, Atlanta, Georgia
DIED	April 4, 1968, Memphis, Tennessee
AGE AT DEATH	39
OTHER NAMES	MLK
FAMILY	Married Coretta Scott in 1953. They had four children.
LANDMARKS	The Lorraine Motel in Memphis, Tennessee, where King was shot to death, re-opened in 1991 as the National Civil Rights Museum.
MILESTONES	1963: March on Washington. 1964: Civil Rights Act
HONORS	1964: Nobel Peace Prize. A federal holiday, the third Monday in January, which was recognized in every state by 1992, commemorates King. 2008: A memorial in Washington, D.C., is scheduled to open.

Did You Know?

- When King told his first-grade teacher he was only five years old, he was barred from school until he was older.
- King was stabbed in 1958 during a book-signing in Harlem by a woman wielding a seven-inch letter opener. Doctors removed the letter opener, and he recovered.
- Then Democratic presidential candidate John F. Kennedy interceded to have King released from jail in October 1960, an action that is credited with helping Kennedy to be elected president.
- FBI director J. Edgar Hoover tried to blackmail King, because he hated his politics.
- The band U2 wrote a hit song about King, "Pride (in the Name of Love)."

HE WAS ARRESTED AND THROWN IN JAIL many times. He faced hundreds of death threats, and his family's home was bombed. But civil rights leader Martin Luther King, Jr., never backed down in his stand against racism. He dedicated his life to achieving equality and justice for all Americans of all colors. "If a man hasn't discovered something that he will die for," King remarked in 1963, "he isn't fit to live."

Born in Atlanta, Georgia, in 1929, King came from a well-to-do family of preachers. Both his father and grandfather were pastors of Ebenezer Baptist Church, one of the most important churches in Atlanta's African-American community.

Like most black southerners of his generation, King experienced racial prejudice early in life. He was about six years old when a white friend announced that his parents would not let him play with King anymore, since they were going to segregated schools. Another time, a clerk in a shoe store insisted that King and his father go to the back of the store to be served. The elder King responded, "We'll either buy shoes sitting here or won't buy any shoes at all." Then he walked out of the store. King took note of his father's proud protest.

Today it's hard to imagine the depth of racial injustice that once existed in the United States. But when King was growing up, segregation was both the law and custom in the South and other parts of America. Blacks could not go to school with white children, vote, serve on juries, sit

Martin Luther King, Jr., (above with his wife, Coretta Scott King) dreamed of an America without racial prejudice, in which his "four little children will one day live in a nation where they will not be judged by the color of their skin but by the content of their character." He devoted his life to making this dream of equality come true.

In 1964 King took time out from his civil rights work to attend the World's Fair in New York City and enjoy the Magic Skyway ride with his children Yolanda and Martin Luther III (above). The same year Congress passed the Civil Rights Act, which outlawed segregation in publicly owned facilities.

anywhere they chose on a bus, or buy or rent a home wherever they wanted. They couldn't be treated at white hospitals, use whites-only restrooms, or eat in the same restaurants as whites. In some parts of the South, African Americans even had to step off the sidewalk if a white person walked by.

King entered Morehouse College in Atlanta at the age of 15. In his senior year he decided to become a minister, in part because he felt "an inner urge to serve humanity." He believed the best way to do that was through the church, which was the strongest black institution. He had learned from his family that religion and politics were a powerful combination.

King graduated from Crozer Theological Seminary in Pennsylvania with the highest grade average in his class and a reputation as a passionate and persuasive speaker. From there he went

to Boston, Massachusetts, where he obtained a doctorate in philosophy from Boston University. While he was in Boston, King met Coretta Scott, a student at the New England Conservatory of Music. They soon found they shared a commitment to changing the racist system they had both grown up under. They married in 1953.

The following year Martin and Coretta, who was pregnant with the first of their four children, moved to Montgomery, Alabama. King became pastor of the Dexter Avenue Baptist Church. In December of 1955, Montgomery's black leadership recruited King to lead a boycott of the city's segregated public bus system. The boycott began when an African-American woman named Rosa Parks (see pages 158–159) refused to give up her bus seat to a white passenger. As a result, she was arrested for breaking the city's segregation law.

The first day of the boycott was held on the

day of Parks's trial. Instead of taking the bus as usual, most black residents walked or carpooled to work. That night more than 4,000 boycott supporters gathered for a meeting at a local church and decided to continue the boycott. When 26-year-old King took the pulpit, he electrified the crowd: "There comes a time," he said, "that people get tired. We are here this evening to say to those who have mistreated us so long that we are tired—tired of being segregated and humiliated, tired of being kicked about by the brutal feet of oppression."

Over the next year, King spoke night after night at rallies in churches. His impassioned sermons inspired the bus boycotters to keep their spirits up, their means peaceful, and their eyes on their goal. Along the way King came to believe that nonviolent resistance—the peaceful refusal to obey an unjust law—was the best way to bring about social change. He preached that "nonviolence can touch men where the law cannot reach them." And to Montgomery's white leaders he directed these words: "We will meet your physical force with soul force. We will not hate you, but we will not obey your evil laws. We will soon wear you down by our capacity to suffer."

During the boycott King was arrested several

> "Injustice anywhere is a threat to justice everywhere."
>
> Letter from Birmingham Jail, April 16, 1963

King posed for this portrait at Atlanta's Ebenezer Baptist Church—where he was co-pastor with his father—in 1964. Jailed (above right) after leading a protest in Birmingham, Alabama, in 1963, King composed a letter to clergy who called his actions "unwise and untimely." In it he reminded them that African Americans "have waited for more than 340 years for our Constitutional and God-given rights."

times on trumped-up charges, and he received death threats that left him shaken. One night a midnight caller threatened: "If you aren't out of this town in three days, we're gonna blow your brains out and blow up your house." King went to his kitchen and prayed, confessing that he was "losing his courage." According to King, he then heard an inner voice saying: "Martin Luther, stand up for righteousness. Stand up for justice. Stand up for truth. And, lo, I will be with you, even until the end of the world." King decided to fight on.

On December 20, 1956, the Montgomery bus boycott ended 382 days after it began, when the United States Supreme Court upheld a ruling that the bus segregation policy was unconstitutional. Inspired by this victory, King and other black clergymen organized the Southern Christian Leadership Conference (SCLC). The SCLC planned to challenge segregation throughout the South, using the same tactics of nonviolence that had proved so successful in Montgomery.

After Montgomery, the attention of the news media transformed King into a symbol of the struggle for civil rights, and the young preacher became famous around the world. In 1959 he and his wife spent a month in India, where King met with followers of Mahatma Gandhi to discuss the principles of nonviolent resistance. By 1960, King was devoting most of his time to the SCLC and the civil rights movement. He traveled the country speaking out against segregation and spreading the message of nonviolent resistance to unjust laws. He led protest marches. In Atlanta he joined black college students in a sit-in at a segregated lunch

The old hymn "We Shall Overcome" became the anthem of the civil rights movement. In March 1965 King and his wife led a black voting rights march (opposite top) from Selma, Alabama, to the state capital in Montgomery.

counter and was arrested once again.

In the spring of 1963, King and the SCLC led a campaign to end segregation in Birmingham, Alabama, one of the most racist and segregated cities in the South. Birmingham police met peaceful protest marchers—many of them teenagers and schoolchildren—with snarling attack dogs and blasting fire hoses. Images of the brutality appeared on front pages of newspapers across the country, and television beamed the crisis into living rooms for everyone to see. Faced with the negative publicity, Birmingham business leaders agreed to many of the SCLC's demands.

Later that year, King joined other civil rights leaders in organizing the March on Washington for Jobs and Freedom. On August 28, 1963, some 250,000 Americans from across the country, including 60,000 white supporters, gathered in front of the Lincoln Memorial in Washington, D.C., to demand equal justice for all citizens. The highlight of the peaceful protest was King's famous "I Have a Dream" speech, in which he declared, "I have a dream that one day this nation will rise up and live out the true meaning of its creed: We hold these truths to be self-evident—that all men are created equal."

King's emotional speech, broadcast on television and printed in papers around the nation, touched the hearts and consciences of people everywhere and boosted public support for civil rights. In 1964 Congress passed the Civil Rights Act, which outlawed racial segregation in publicly owned facilities. In December of that same year, King received the Nobel Peace Prize.

> "When the architects of our republic wrote the magnificent words of the Constitution and the Declaration of Independence, they were signing a promissory note to which every American was to fall heir....Instead of honoring this sacred obligation, America has given the Negro people a bad check."

March on Washington speech, August 28, 1963

Over the next few years, King looked on in sorrow as younger activists rejected his philosophy of nonviolence and riots broke out in the ghettoes of several big cities. He began to focus on economic inequality as well as racial discrimination. He wanted to form a coalition of poor people of all races to address issues of poverty.

In 1968 King went to Memphis, Tennessee, to help support a strike by the city's sanitation workers. On April 4, 1968, as he relaxed on the balcony of his room

On the 30th anniversary of King's death, people marched in Memphis to pay tribute to the man and his ideas.

at the Lorraine Motel, King was assassinated by a white racist named James Earl Ray. In a speech given the night before he died, King spoke these prophetic words: "Like anybody, I would like to live a long life...but I'm not concerned about that now. I just want to do God's will. And He's allowed me to go up to the mountain. And I've looked over, and I've seen the promised land. I may not get there with you, but I want you to know tonight that we as a people will get to the promised land."

Roberto Clemente

BORN August 18, 1934, Carolina, Puerto Rico

DIED December 31, 1972, San Juan, Puerto Rico

AGE AT DEATH 38

OTHER NAMES Called "Arriba" in his native Puerto Rico

FAMILY Father: Melcor Clemente (cleh-MEN-tay), a foreman at a sugar mill. Mother: Luisa Walker

LANDMARKS National Baseball Hall of Fame, Cooperstown, New York. Roberto Clemente Sports City, a 304-acre sports complex, Carolina, Puerto Rico

MILESTONES September 30, 1972: In his last at-bat, on the final day of the regular season, Clemente hit a double off the New York Mets' Jon Matlack, at Pittsburgh's Three Rivers Stadium, for his 3,000th career hit. It was his last regular season time at bat, and his last hit.

HONORS 2003: Presidential Medal of Freedom (posthumous)

Did You Know?

- The Hall of Fame waived its traditional five-year waiting period after a player's death or retirement for Clemente, and Clemente was elected to the Hall with 93 percent of the vote. He was inducted in 1973. He was also the first player of Latin American descent to be inducted into the Hall of Fame.
- The Roberto Clemente Foundation estimates that over the last 31 years, 300,000 children have taken part in its programs, which have involved such players as Ivan Rodriguez, Bernie Williams, Benito Santiago, and Juan Gonzalez.

ON THE BASEBALL FIELD, right fielder Roberto Clemente stood out for his explosive batting, his aggressive base running, his spectacular catches, and his precise and powerful throws. Off the field, he won widespread admiration for his dedication to his Latin American heritage and his commitment to public service.

Clemente was born in Carolina, Puerto Rico. As a teenager, he played on one of Puerto Rico's Winter League teams along with players from the American Negro leagues and the major leagues, who often came to Puerto Rico to play in the off-season.

After graduating from high school in 1954, Clemente signed with the Brooklyn Dodgers, who sent him to the minor leagues. The following year he was drafted by the Pittsburgh Pirates. He stayed with them for the rest of his career and became a baseball superstar. He won 12 Gold Gloves for his excellence in the outfield, made the All-Star team 12 times, and led the National League in batting four times. In 1960 and 1971, he helped lead the Pirates to World Series championships.

Clemente spoke out against the double prejudice faced by Latin American black ballplayers. "Because they speak Spanish among themselves," he said, "they are set off as a minority within a minority." He went back to Puerto Rico to play in the winter leagues so that local fans could watch him. He believed it was important for young Latinos to have role models. After an earthquake ravaged Nicaragua in December 1972, Clemente headed for the country with relief supplies. He was killed when his plane crashed into the sea soon after takeoff.

In 1973 Roberto Clemente was inducted into the Baseball Hall of Fame. At the ceremony, the baseball commissioner praised him: "He was so very great a man, as a leader and humanitarian, so very great an inspiration to the young and to all in baseball, especially to the proud people of his homeland, Puerto Rico."

Baseball great Roberto Clemente was known for his unorthodox hitting style. "He's the strangest hitter in baseball," said former L.A. Dodgers pitcher Sandy Koufax. "Figure him one way and he'll kill you another." Clemente is remembered today for his humanitarian efforts as well as his extraordinary baseball skills.

César Chávez

BORN	March 31, 1927, Yuma, Arizona
DIED	April 23, 1993, San Luis, Arizona
AGE AT DEATH	66
OTHER NAMES	César Estrada Chávez (birth name)
FAMILY	Father: Librado Chávez. Mother: Juana Estrada. Married Helen Fabela in 1948. They had eight children.
LANDMARKS	June 2000: César E. Chávez Plaza in Sacramento, California, was dedicated. At Sonoma State University's library, there is a César Chávez Memorial Mural.
HONORS	1974: Martin Luther King Nonviolent Peace Award. 1994: Presidential Medal of Freedom (posthumous).

Did You Know?

- Chávez's mother, Juana, originally inspired his devotion to nonviolence. From her, he learned hundreds of *dichos* (proverbs), which he used throughout his life.
- As a young man he was influenced by books on labor leaders such as John L. Lewis and Eugene Debs. He also read political philosophy. He was most influenced by the writings of Mahatma Gandhi.
- For the most part, César Chávez lived as simply and poorly as the workers he represented. He never owned a house or a car, and he never earned more than $6,000 a year.
- In 1975, the law that Chávez and the UFW had fought so long for—the Agricultural Labor Relations Act, which provided greater rights for farmworkers and their representatives—was passed in California.

THE GREAT LABOR AND CIVIL RIGHTS LEADER César Chávez knew exactly what life was like for poor Mexican-American farmworkers. He spent many years toiling for low wages in the fruit and vegetable fields of California. The rest of his time he dedicated to improving the lives of his fellow workers.

César Chávez was born near Yuma, Arizona, in 1927. His parents, Librado and Juana Chávez, owned a farm and a small general store. César grew up with plenty to eat, and he went to school regularly. When he was ten years old, however, all that changed. His parents lost their property, like countless other people during the Great Depression. The Chávez family moved to California, where they became migrant workers—people who move from region to region to harvest crops.

César and his family never stayed anywhere for long. In the winter, for example, they picked carrots and peas in one part of the state. In spring they moved on to melon fields somewhere else. Come August they tended tomatoes and grapes in still another place, then they traveled to cotton fields in the fall. To help earn money for the family, the children pitched in when they weren't in school. When they were, César and his siblings often faced discrimination from teachers who were prejudiced against Spanish-speaking students. In all, César attended some 30 different schools in California.

César Chávez made it his mission to improve the lives of poor migrant farmworkers. The union he helped create, the United Farm Workers, used boycotts (advertised above) to gain support for workers' demands for fair wages and better working conditions. In 1986 Chávez kicked off a new grape boycott (left) to protest the use of toxic pesticides by grape growers.

Living conditions for migrant workers like César's family were terrible. Because they moved so often, most migrants had no home of their own. They slept in cars, in tents, or in crowded camps built by farm owners. The shacks in such camps usually lacked electricity, running water, and indoor bathrooms. Such unsanitary conditions made people sick. To make matters worse, migrant workers were very poorly paid for their backbreaking labor. Their families often went hungry. Workers who dared to complain were fired—there were plenty of penniless immigrants to take their place.

In 1968 César Chávez went on a 25-day public fast to dramatize the suffering of farmworkers and encourage Americans to boycott California grapes. U.S. Senator Robert F. Kennedy (above left) joined Chávez when he finally broke his fast. Senator Kennedy called Chávez "one of the heroic figures of our time."

Chávez went back to the farm labor circuit. Meanwhile, he began reading and thinking about what he could do to change the horrible way in which farmworkers were treated.

In 1952 Chávez started working for a civil rights group called the Community Service Organization. He helped Mexican Americans become U.S. citizens and register to vote, and he helped them protest discrimination in schools, jobs, and housing. As the years passed he became more concerned than ever about the plight of migrant workers, who had little protection from the abuses of greedy farm owners. He decided the best way to help them was to organize a union.

César Chávez left school after eighth grade to work full-time in the fields. A few years later he joined the U.S. Navy. When his tour of duty ended, he returned to California. In 1948 he married Helen Fabela, who also came from a migrant family. The following year the first of their eight children was born. To support his growing family,

With the help of Mexican-American community activist Dolores Huerta, in 1962 Chávez founded the union that would become the United Farm Workers (UFW). Three years later, Chávez and the UFW began a strike against grape growers in the Delano, California, area. They demanded more

"Our boycotts are predicated on faith
in the basic compassion of people everywhere.
We are convinced that when consumers are faced with
a direct appeal from the poor struggling against great odds,
they will react positively.
The American people still yearn for justice."

article by Chávez in *Los Angeles Times,* January 2, 1975

pay and better treatment for migrant workers. The UFW also asked American citizens everywhere to boycott grapes from California until the growers agreed to bargain with the union.

To gain public support for the union's cause, known as "La Causa," Chávez relied on tactics of nonviolent resistance. "Nonviolence takes more guts...than violence," he explained. "Nonviolence is hard work. It is the willingness to sacrifice. It is the patience to win." He led a march from Delano to the steps of the state capitol in Sacramento, 340 miles away. By the end of the walk, Chávez's feet were blistered and bloody, but the national media attention the event received led one of the big grape growers to sign a contract with the union. Later Chávez went on a month-long fast to dramatize the suffering of farmworkers. Inspired by his sacrifice, millions of Americans rallied to the cause and stopped buying grapes. The growers bowed to the pressure, and by 1970 a majority of them had signed contracts with the UFW. The union, which had swelled to 50,000 members by this time, lifted the boycott.

Over the next two decades, Chávez continued to lead the struggle for farmworkers' rights. In time the UFW won higher wages for agricultural workers as well as improved working conditions. In 1988, when he was 61 years old, Chávez undertook another public fast, this time to draw attention to the deadly effects pesticides were having on farmworkers and their children.

When César Chávez died in 1993, some 50,000 mourners attended his funeral Mass. People across America paid tribute to the gentle, courageous, and charismatic man who raised the consciousness of the nation.

Chávez took to the streets in 1976 to campaign for a proposition that would benefit farmworkers. A disciple of nonviolent resistance, he led the struggle for farmworkers' rights until his death.

Daniel K. Inouye

★

BORN September 7, 1924, Honolulu, Hawaii

FAMILY Father: Hyotaro Inouye (in-YOU-eh). Mother: Kame Inouye. He is the eldest of four children. Married Margaret Shinobu Awamura in 1948

LANDMARKS Daniel K. Inouye Building at the Walter Reed Army Institute of Research, Bethesda, Maryland

MILESTONES 1954: Inouye began his political career. He was elected to the Hawaii Territorial House of Representatives.

HONORS 2000: Congressional Medal of Honor. The Pasadena Cherry Blossom Festival in Pasadena, California, offers the Senator Daniel Inouye Leadership Award. December 2005: the National Defense University Foundation's American Patriot Award

Did You Know?

- The soldiers of the 442nd Regimental Combat Team, of which Senator Inouye was a leader, and 100th Battalion, organized in Hawaii, were among the most decorated and honored units of their size in the history of the Army. They were awarded with 20 Medals of Honor, 52 Distinguished Service Crosses, 560 Silver Stars, 4,000 Bronze Stars, and 9,486 Purple Hearts.

- For his work on behalf of Native Americans, Senator Inouye was awarded the first ever National Center First American Congressional Advocate Award. He was cited for his continued dedication to increasing economic opportunities among Native Americans.

BORN AND RAISED IN HONOLULU, Daniel K. Inouye was a *nisei,* a child of Japanese immigrants. He was 17 when the Japanese attacked Pearl Harbor on December 7, 1941. "Like all nisei," he recalled, "I was driven by an insidious sense of guilt from the instant the first Japanese plane appeared over Pearl Harbor. Of course we had nothing to feel guilty about, but we all carried this special burden."

Eager to join the war effort and prove his loyalty to the United States, Inouye left college in 1943 to enlist in the U.S. Army's 442nd Regimental Combat Team—an all-volunteer unit made up of Japanese-American soldiers. It became the most decorated unit for its size in U.S. military history. In Italy near the end of the war, Second Lieutenant Inouye led his platoon in an assault against a heavily fortified German position on a hill. Though severely wounded during the action, he continued to lead the attack until the hill was captured.

After the battle, Inouye's right arm had to be amputated. He spent the next 20 months in the hospital recovering from his injuries. His "extraordinary heroism" earned him more than a dozen medals and citations.

While Inouye and his regiment risked their lives overseas to preserve our democratic freedom, at home the United States took away the civil rights of Japanese Americans. Concerned that they might aid the enemy, the government forced more than 100,000 Japanese Americans living along the West Coast to move to internment camps in Wyoming, Utah, and other western states.

After the war, Inouye graduated from the University of Hawaii. He went to law school with the goal of entering public life. When Hawaii became the 50th state in 1959, Inouye was elected the island's first member of the House of Representatives. In 1962 Hawaiians voted him to the U.S. Senate, where he still serves.

U.S. Senator Daniel K. Inouye, a Democrat, hopes Americans will remember the values that his regiment and other segregated units that fought in World War II represented: "That patriotism and love of our great country are not limited to any ethnic group, and wartime hysteria must never again lead us to trample on our democratic principles."

HEROES OF TODAY

★ *Inspiring Individuals* ★

Many of the Americans featured in this book were proclaimed heroes in their own time. Others did not receive recognition until long after their death. All of these men and women, however, have stood up to the test of history. Looking back, we can see that they all made a positive and lasting difference to American society, in ways that still inspire us today.

But as historian Robert D. Johnston mentioned in his introduction, it was not easy coming up with a list of historical heroes that everyone involved in this project could agree upon. It is even harder to identify which of those Americans who are admired today will be recognized as heroes 20, 50, or 200 years from now.

Most Americans agree that the firefighters, police officers, members of the military, and ordinary citizens who act bravely in times of crisis are heroes, even if few of their individual names will make it into the history books of tomorrow. People who invent or discover things that help others or who revolutionize

Named Time *magazine's first "hero for the planet," marine biologist Sylvia Earle has pioneered research on marine ecosystems. She is a key advocate for conservation of the world's oceans.*

Perhaps the world's richest man, Microsoft co-founder Bill Gates and his wife, Melinda Gates, have donated billions of dollars to bring "innovations in health and learning to the global community."

Architect Maya Lin's design for the Vietnam Veterans Memorial in Washington, D.C., initially caused controversy. It is now thought one of the nation's most powerful monuments.

Texan Barbara Jordan triumphed over racism and sexism when she became the first African-American woman from the Deep South elected to the U.S. Congress. She served from 1972 to 1978.

When Ellen Ochoa was accepted into NASA's training program in 1990, she became the first Hispanic woman in the astronaut corps. Since then she has flown three space shuttle missions.

technology earn our esteem. So do those who triumph over adversity against all odds. Many of us also admire the female and minority trailblazers in areas once largely reserved for white males, such as space exploration, the United States Senate, and the Indy 500.

In general, however, today's heroes are largely a matter of personal taste. My eighth-grade English teacher, Mrs. Ellington, is a hero of mine for drilling into me the rules of grammar and punctuation and for encouraging me to write. Rock star Bruce Springsteen—the "Boss"—is a favorite of Robert Johnston, both for his stirring music and because "he believes in embracing, very openly and directly, the outcasts of our society."

Some of today's most popular heroes are famous athletes or musicians or other superstars. The best of these people inspire us not only with their talent but with their hearts and their guts, their commitment to excellence, and their dedication to their sport or to their craft. Sometimes, however, celebrities are idolized just because they are famous, and the super rich are revered just because they have so much money. In today's world, fame and heroism are often confused.

It's up to you to decide who your own American heroes are and why they deserve your admiration. You can find them in all walks of life. Heroism is not limited by gender or race or culture or occupation or age. The people shown below are all greatly admired today, for a variety of reasons. Two of them are kids. Whether any of these people will become heroes of American history is something that only time will tell, but in the meantime we can all be uplifted and inspired by their example.

> "Those who say that we are in a time when there are no heroes just don't know where to look."
>
> President Ronald Reagan,
> First Inaugural Address, 1981

Star of the Superman movies, actor Christopher Reeve showed true courage when he became an activist for medical research after a 1995 accident left him a quadriplegic.

Ten-year-old Samantha Smith inspired the world in 1982 when she wrote a letter to the Soviet leader and was invited to visit him. Her trip came to symbolize the hope for peace.

Mattie Stepanek's moving poetry and courageous spirit in the face of fatal illness earned him the admiration of countless Americans. He died in 2004 at the age of 13.

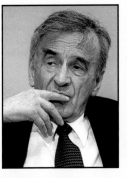

Nobel Peace Prize winner and author Elie Wiesel survived the Nazi death camps of the Holocaust as a teenager. He has made it his life's work to ensure that such a thing never happens again.

Golfer Tiger Woods wins fans—and millions in prize money—with his amazing talent and commitment to the game. Off the greens, he supports programs for children's health and education.

INDEX

QUOTE SOURCES

Page 10: *With Courage and Cloth,* by Ann Bausum (WCC), p. 15; Page 13: *American Heritage History of the United States,* by Douglas Brinkley (AHH), p. 1; Page 15: *Eyewitness to America,* edited by David Colbert (ETA), p. 19; Page 17: AHH, p.38; Page 19: both quotes from www.harvardmagazine.com/one-line/1102194.html; "a woman of haughty..." www.greatwomen.org/women.php?action=viewone&id=84; Page 23: "a better ..." *American National Biography* (ANB), p. 382; "But being ..." ANB, p.384; "They that ..." *Bartlett's Familiar Quotations,* p. 310; Page 24: ANB, p.384; Page 25: "river in..." ANB, p.389; "Lose no..." *Benjamin Franklin,* by Edmund S. Morgan, p. 23; "If you..." ANB, p. 394; Page 26: "We must ..." *Bartlett's,* p. 310; "Fish..." and "As we..." www.pbs.org/benfranklin/; Page 27: both quotes from www.pbs.org/benfranklin/; Page 34: "I think..." http://gwpapers.virginia.edu/revolution/letters/bfairfax2.html; "Observe good..." *Bartlett's,* p.336; Page 35: "There was in his..." and "First in war..." www.pbs.org/georgewashington/; "With slight..." *The Making of America,* by Robert Johnston (MOA), p. 59; Page 37: "In the new..." *Bartlett's,* p. 347; "As to your..." http://www.masshist.org/adams/quotes.cfm; Page 39: ETA, p. 98; Page 41: "to declare the..." and "Declaration of Rights..." www.yale.edu/lawweb/avalon/const/const02.htm; Page 43: "It is easy..." ETA, p. 98; "that he would..." ANB, p. 647; "The security..." and "As much..." and "I am truly..." http://gunstonhall.org/georgemason/; Page 45: "those western..." and "If therefore..." and "Dear Lewis..." *How We Crossed the West,* by Rosalyn Schanzer; "was remarkable..." *Lewis & Clark,* by Stephen E. Ambrose (L&C), p. 28; Page 46: L&C p. 175; Page 47: L&C, p. 97; Page 48: Schanzer; Page 49: L&C, p. 98; Page 51: "A woman..." NATIONAL GEOGRAPHIC MAGAZINE, Feb. 2003, p. 79; "great waters" L&C, p.183; Page 53: All quotes from *Bartlett's,* page 369-370; Page 57: "The right..." www.nps.gov/wori/address.htm; "discuss the..." WCC, p. 18; Page 59: both quotes from *Perseverance,* p. 63; Page 62: both quotes from www.africanamericans.com/FBIBlackHistoryMonth.htm; Page 63: "a live..." www.nyhistory.com/harriettubman/life.htm; "You'll be..." and "never lost..." www.pbs.org/wgbh/aia/part4/4p1535.html; Page 66: "Often limb..." *Our Country's Presidents,* by Ann Bausum (OCP), p. 74; "If I..." Encyclopedia Britannica Online (EBO); Page 69: both quotes from ANB, p. 290; Page 71: "freedom of..." *Yankee Women,* by Elizabeth D. Leonard (YW), p. 109; "herself with ..." www.medalofhonor.com/; "The greatest..." YW, p. 109; "depraved Yankee..." YW, p. 139; Page 73: "Remember that..." http://tomscourses.tripod.com/abolit1.htm; "those who..." *Don't Know Much About History,* by Kenneth C. Davis (DKM), p. 195; Page 74: *Bartlett's,* p. 480; Page 75: "The existence..." *The Nation,* 7/19/2004; "Agitate..." ANB, p. 819; Page 77: *Rabble Rousers,* by Cheryl Harness (RR),

p. 23; Page 78: WCC, p.18; Page 79: ANB, p. 548; Page 80: *Bartlett's,* p. 475; Page 81: "not a..." ANB, p. 550; "Failure..." www.pbs.org/stantonanthony/; "Marriage..." *Bartlett's,* p. 492; Page 83: DKM, p. 259; Page 87: *Bartlett's,* p. 516; Page 89: "Treat all..." and "We ask..." *The Native Americans,* by David Hurst Thomas (NA), p.352; "Hear me..." *Bartlett's,* p. 541; Page 91: "I fairly..." *The Many Lives of Andrew Carnegie,* by Milton Meltzer, p. 25; "The man..." www.pbs.org/wgbh/amex/carnegie/filmmore/description.html; Page 92: Meltzer, p. 58; Page 93: "Upon the..." DKM, p. 271; "[take] a part..." Meltzer, p. 63; Page 97: "the world..." and "The study..." *Always Inventing,* by Tom L. Matthews (AI), pp. 55 and 48; Page 98: www.pbs.org/sgbh/amex/telephone/peopleevents/mabell.html; Page 99: "I think..." AI, p, 23; "Mr. Watson..." AI, p. 27; "I believe..." http://www.biographi.ca/EN/ShowBio.asp?BioId=42027; Page 100: "to follow ..." AI, p. 33; Page 101: "for all..." NATIONAL GEOGRAPHIC MAGAZINE, 9/1988, p. 380; "can no..." AI, p. 5; "brought the..." AI, p. 500; "The inventor..." http://www.biographi.ca/EN/ShowBio.asp?BioId=42027; Page 103: www.cr.nps.gov/museum/exhibits/tuskegee/gwcteach.htm; Page 105: *National Geographic Almanac of World History,* by Patricia S. Daniels, p. 274; Page 107: *Airborne,* by Mary Collins, p. 9; Page 109: Collins, p. 5; Page 111: AHH, p. 331; Page 113: www2.pfeiffer.edu/~Iridener/DSS/Addams/2hh1.html; Page 115: all quotes from news.nationalgeographic.com/news/2003/01/0110_030113_henson.html; Page 117: "The problem..." MOA, p. 135; "to make..." EBO; Page 119: all quotes from *Leadership,* p. 223; Page 121: "When we..." www2.nytimes.com/specials/magazine4/articles/keller1.html; "Sometimes I..." Time 100 web site; "When we..." *Helen Keller: A Determined Life,* by Elizabeth Macleod, p. 22; Page 122: "soul's birthday" http://www.perkins.org/museum/section.php?id=218; "The most ..." and "As the cool..." www2.nytimes.com/specials/magazine4/articles/keller1.html; Page 123: *Bartlett's,* p. 641; Page 125: WCC, p. 40; Page 127: *An American Hero: The True Story of Charles A. Lindbergh,* by Barry Denenberg, p. 310; "I saw..." *Bartlett's,* p. 709; "the British..." Denenberg, p. 213; "the forerunner..." Denenberg, p. 94; Page 131: www.ameliaearhart.com/about/index/php; Page 132: "As soon..." ANB, p. 222; "to prove..." *Sky Pioneer,* by Corinne Szabo, p. 27; Page 133: Szabo, p. 58; Page 135: Time 100; Page 136: "new deal ..." and "The only..." OCP, p. 130; "The test..." Bartlett's, p. 649; Page 137: "traitor ..." Time 100; "all aid..." MOA, p. 154; Page 139: www.cmgww.com/historic/malcolm/about/quotes_articles.htm; Page 141: *Genius,* by Marfé Ferguson Delano, p.14; Page 143: *Bartlett's,* p. 635; Page 145: "never doubted..." *The Autobiography of Eleanor Roosevelt* (AER), p. 6; "was always..." AER, p. 12; "The feeling..." ANB, p. 812; Page 146: "starting a.." AER, p. 24; "saw little..." *Eleanor Roosevelt: A Life of*

Discovery, by Russell Freedman, p. 34; "I was always..." AER, p. 62; Page 147: "As I saw..." AER, p. 163; "You gain..." *Bartlett's,* p. 654; Page 148: Freedman, p. 110; Page 149: "No one..." *Bartlett's,* p. 654; "Everyone..." Freedman, p. 111; Page 151: "had never..." *Margaret Mead,* by Edra Ziesk, p. 13; "unknown ways..." and "onslaught..." Ziesk, p. 14; "I have spent..." www.medaloffreedom.com/MargaretMead.htm; "attempt to ..." Ziesk, p. 21; "never doubt that..." www.mead2001.org/faq_page.htm; Page 153: "beauty of ..." and "hysterical woman" Time 100; "Over increasingly..." *Silent Spring,* by Rachel Carson, chapter 8. Page 155: *Human Rights Great Lives,* by William Jay Jacobs, p. 193; Page 156: www.thurgoodmarshall.com/speeches/tmlaw_article.htm; Page 157: "In light of..." www.thurgoodmarshall.com/speeches/tmlaw_article.htm; "Equal means..." www.arlingtoncemetery.net/tmarsh.htm; Page 159: *Encyclopedia of African-American Culture and History* (EAACH), p. 2103; Page 161: ANB, p. 212; Page 164: "Plenty of ..." EBO; "Mr. Rickey,.." and "Robinson, I'm..." *I Never Had It Made,* by Jackie Robinson, p. 34; "all adventure..." "The Jackie Robinson I Remember," by Roger Kahn in *The Journal of Blacks in Higher Education,* Winter 1996/1997, p.88; "had not been ..." Robinson, p. 34; Page 165: "has demonstrated..." and "Back in the..." *Jackie Robinson,* by Arnold Rampersand, p. 7; Page 167: *John Glenn: Space Pioneer,* by Carmen Bredeson, p. 7; Page 169: "The white..." *Autobiography of Malcolm X,* p. 312; "freedom by..." MOA, p. 171; Page 170: "I'm for truth..." http://www.malcolm-x.org/quotes.htm; "we are black..." EAACH, p. 1683; Page 171: "Concerning..." www.cmgww.com/historic/malcolm/about/quotes_by.htm; "by any means..." MOA, p. 171; "We were al..." *Malcolm X,* by Walter Dean Myer; "It is a time..." http://www.africawithin.com/malcolmx/quotes.htm; Page 173: "If a man..." *Bartlett's,* p. 760; "We'll either buy..." http://www.stanford.edu/group/King/publications/autobiography/ch_1.htm; "four little..." *Bartlett's,* p. 761; Page 175: "There comes..." *Perseverance,* p. 192; "Injustice anywhere..." and "Perhaps it is easy..." http://www.nobelprizes.com/nobel/peace/MLK-jail.html; "nonviolence can..." *Martin Luther King, Jr.,* by Marshall Frady, p. 40; "We will meet..." Frady, p. 39; Page 176: "If you aren't..." and "Martin Luther, stand..." Time 100; "I have a dream..." MOA, p. 169; Page 177: "When the architects..." www.usconstitution.net/dream.html; "Like anybody..." *Bartlett's,* p. 761; Page 179: "Because they speak..." ANB, p. 52; "He was so very..." and "He's the strangest..." www.latinosportslegends.com/clemente.htm; Page 182: www.sfsu.edu/~cecipp/cesar_chavez/Union_Is_Alive.htm; Page 183: *Cesar Chavez: Fighter in the Fields,* by J. L. Matthews, p. 35; Page 185: "Like all nisei..." *Contemporary Heroes and Heroines,* p. 280; "That patriotism..." http://inouye.senate.gov/biography.html; Page 187: MOA, p. 188.

RESOURCE GUIDE

A variety of books, Web sites, and magazine and newspaper articles were consulted for this book. Below are some of the sources I found most helpful.

BOOKS

Ambrose, Stephen E. *Lewis & Clark: Voyage of Discovery.* Washington, D.C.: National Geographic Society, 1998.

Bartlett, John. *Bartlett's Familiar Quotations,* 16th ed. Boston: Little Brown & Company, 1992.

Bausum, Ann. *Our Country's Presidents.* Washington, D.C.: National Geographic Society, 2001.

_____. *With Courage and Cloth: Winning the Fight for a Woman's Right to Vote.* Washington, D.C.: National Geographic Society, 2004.

Brinkley, Douglas. *American Heritage History of the United States.* New York: Viking, 1998.

Colbert, David, editor. *Eyewitness to America: 500 Years of America in the Words of Those Who Saw It Happen.* New York: Pantheon Books, 1997.

Daniels, Patricia S., and Stephen G. Hyslop. *National Geographic Almanac of World History.* Washington, D.C.: National Geographic Society, 2003.

Davis, Kenneth C. *Don't Know Much About History.* New York: HarperCollins, 2003.

Deford, Frank. *The Heart of a Champion: Celebrating the Spirit and Character of Great American Sports Heroes.* San Diego: Tehabi Books, 2002.

Delano, Marfé Ferguson. *Genius: A Photobiography of Albert Einstein.* Washington, D.C.: National Geographic Society, 2005.

Denenberg, Dennis, and Lorraine Roscoe. *50 American Heroes Every Kid Should Meet.* Brookfield, CT: The Millbrook Press, 2001.

Faber, Doris, and Harold Faber. *American Government Great Lives.* New York: Charles Scribner's Sons, 1988.

Freidel, Frank. *The Presidents of the United States of America.* Washington, D.C.: White House Historical Association, 1995.

Garraty, John A. and Mark C. Carnes, editors. *American National Biography.* New York: Oxford University Press, 1999.

Jacobs, William Jay. *Human Rights Great Lives.* New York: Charles Scribner's Sons, 1990.

Johnston, Robert D. *The Making of America: The History of the United States from 1492 to the Present.* Washington, D.C.: National Geographic Society, 2002.

Keenan, Sheila. *Scholastic Book of Outstanding Americans: Profiles of More Than 450 Famous and Infamous Figures in U.S. History.* New York: Scholastic Reference, 2003.

Leadership. African Americans: Voices of Triumph series. Time-Life Books. Alexandria, Va: Time-Life Books, 1993.

Perseverance. African Americans: Voices of Triumph series. Time-Life Books. Alexandria, Va: Time-Life Books, 1993.

Rubel, David. *Scholastic Encyclopedia of the Presidents and Their Times.* New York: Scholastic Inc., 1994.

Thomas, David Hurst, et. al. *The Native Americans: An Illustrated History.* Atlanta: Turner Publishing, Inc., 1993.

Virga, Vincent. *Eyes of the Nation: A Visual History of the United States.* New York: Alfred A. Knopf, 1997.

War for the Plains. The American Indians series. Time-Life Books. Alexandria, Va.: Time-Life Books, 1994.

Ware, Susan, editor. *Forgotten Heroes: Inspiring American Portraits from Our Leading Historians.* New York: The Free Press, 1998.

WEB SITES

American Experience. PBS Online. http://www.pbs.org/wgbh/amex/index.html Includes biographies of several of the heroes profiled in this book.

American Memory Timeline. The Learning Page. The Library of Congress. http://memory.loc.gov/ammem/ndlpedu/features/timeline/index.html A great source for key events in American history.

Encyclopedia Britannica Online. www.britannica.com

Smithsonian Education—Students Home Page. Smithsonian Institution. http://smithsonianeducation.org/students/index.html Explores people and places, history and culture.

Spotlight: Biography. Smithsonian Institution. http://smithsonianeducation.org/spotlight/start.html Profiles of famous and not-so-famous Americans.

Time 100: The Most Important People of the Century. http://www.time.com/time/time100/ Includes articles on several of the heroes profiled in this book.

CREDITS

National Geographic Society

John M. Fahey, Jr.
PRESIDENT AND CHIEF EXECUTIVE OFFICER

Gilbert M. Grosvenor
CHAIRMAN OF THE BOARD

Nina D. Hoffman
EXECUTIVE VICE PRESIDENT, PRESIDENT OF BOOKS
AND EDUCATION PUBLISHING GROUP

Ericka Markman
SENIOR VICE PRESIDENT, PRESIDENT OF CHILDREN'S
BOOKS AND EDUCATION PUBLISHING GROUP

Stephen Mico
PUBLISHER, VICE PRESIDENT OF CHILDREN'S BOOKS
AND EDUCATION PUBLISHING GROUP

Staff for this book:
Nancy Laties Feresten
VICE PRESIDENT, EDITOR-IN-CHIEF OF CHILDREN'S BOOKS

Bea Jackson
DESIGN DIRECTOR, CHILDREN'S BOOKS AND EDUCATION
PUBLISHING GROUP

Margaret Sidlosky
ILLUSTRATIONS DIRECTOR, CHILDREN'S BOOKS AND
EDUCATION PUBLISHING GROUP

Jennifer Emmett
PROJECT EDITOR

**Daniel L. Sherman, David M. Seager,
Ruth Thompson**
DESIGNERS

Jamie Rose
ILLUSTRATIONS EDITOR

Michelle R. Harris
RESEARCHER

Priyanka Lamichhane
EDITORIAL ASSISTANT

Janet Dustin, Jean Cantu
ILLUSTRATIONS COORDINATORS

Rebecca Barns, Lise Sajewski
COPY EDITORS

Connie D. Binder
INDEXER

Rebecca E. Hinds
MANAGING EDITOR

Jeff Reynolds
MARKETING DIRECTOR, CHILDREN'S BOOKS

R. Gary Colbert
PRODUCTION DIRECTOR

Lewis R. Bassford
PRODUCTION MANAGER

Vincent P. Ryan
MANUFACTURING MANAGER

AUTHOR Marfé Ferguson Delano has written 13
books for National Geographic including *Genius:
A Photobiography of Albert Einstein,* and *Inventing
the Future: A Photobiography of Thomas Alva Edison,*
which received the James Madison Book Award
Honor and was named an ALA Notable book.

For Allie, with love
— MFD

★ ★ ★

Acknowledgments:
The publisher gratefully acknowledges the kind assistance of Wendy Woodfill, Senior Juvenile Selection Librarian, Hennepin County Library; Kathleen Baxter, Acquisitions Librarian and Supervisor of Youth Services, Anoka County Library, Blaine, Minnesota; and Jeanette Larson, Youth Services Manager, Austin Public Library, Texas, for helping to formulate the list of heroes profiled in the book. We appreciate the research assistance of the Franklin Institute, Jill Jackson of the Lewis and Clark Trail Heritage Foundation, Dr. Brendan McConville of Boston University, and Gregory Geddes and Gaylynn Welch of Binghamton University. We're grateful for the photographic research assistance of Mark Renovich from the Franklin Delano Roosevelt Library and Dana Chivvas. Special thanks to Sandy and Isaac Johnston who reviewed the book from a young reader's perspective and provided excellent feedback.

Consultants:
Dr. Robert D. Johnston is Associate Professor and Director of the Teaching of History Program at the University of Illinois at Chicago. He is also the author of National Geographic's *The Making of America: The History of the United States from 1492 to the Present,* which was named a *School Library Journal* Best Book of the Year.

Penelope Harper is a curriculum consultant in Binghamton, New York. She's a Staff Associate at the Center for Teaching American History, Binghamton University, and runs content-based school workshops and reading groups for high school history teachers.

The type for this book is set in Hoefler Text.
Design by Bea Jackson

Printed in the United States of America

Library of Congress Cataloging-in-Publication Information is available from the Library of Congress upon request.
Trade ISBN: 0-7922-7208-0
Library Binding ISBN: 0-7922-7215-3

Front cover: (top) Martin Luther King addressing the crowd at the March on Washington, 1963; (bottom, from left to right) Sacagawea, Amelia Earhart, Albert Einstein, John Glenn.
Title page: A statue in Arlington, Virginia, overlooking the Washington, D.C., skyline commemorates the 1945 World War II Marine victory at Iwo Jima.

The world's largest nonprofit scientific and educational organization, the National Geographic Society was founded in 1888 "for the increase and diffusion of geographic knowledge." Since then it has supported scientific exploration and spread information to its more than nine million members worldwide.

The National Geographic Society educates and inspires millions every day through magazines, books, television programs, videos, maps and atlases, research grants, the National Geographic Bee, teacher workshops, and innovative classroom materials.

The Society is supported through membership dues and income from the sale of its educational products. Members receive NATIONAL GEOGRAPHIC magazine—the Society's official journal—discounts on Society products, and other benefits.

For more information about the National Geographic Society and its educational programs and publications, please call 1-800-NGS-LINE (647-5463), or write to the following address:

National Geographic Society
1145 17th Street N.W.
Washington, D.C. 20036-4688 U.S.A.

Visit the Society's Web site: www.nationalgeographic.com